BEYOND THE GOVERNMENT-HAUNTED WORLD

A COMIC GUIDE TO VOLUNTARYISM, FREE MARKETS, AND THE NON-AGGRESSION PRINCIPLE

ZANDER MARZ

WRITING, ART, AND LETTERING

WRITING, ART, AND LETTERING
ZANDER MARZ

Published by Inspired Arts Press
Worldwide in Cyberspace
www.inspiredartspress.com

First Printing: 2013
10 9 8 7 6 5 4 3 2 1

Library of Congress Control Number Available

Subject Headings: Graphic Novels, Philosophy, Government

ISBN 10: 0982923090
ISBN 13: 978-0-9829230-9-2

Inspired Arts

WORLDWIDE IN CYBERSPACE
PUBLISHING FOR THE 21ST CENTURY

TABLE OF CONTENTS

CHAPTER ZERO

THE GHOST

HELLO, MY NAME IS **ZANDER** AND I'M HERE TO TELL YOU A GHOST STORY. THIS IS A TRUE GHOST STORY.

YEP, I'M NOT KIDDING. IT'S TRUE. AS TRUE AS ANY TRUE GHOST STORY ANYWAY. IT'S BASICALLY A GHOST STORY ABOUT A LONG DEAD SLAVE MASTER THAT JUST WON'T GIVE IT UP.

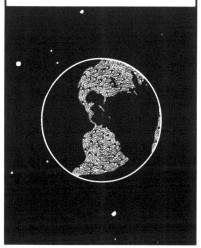

THE GHOST IN THIS STORY IS A GHOST THAT HAUNTS NEARLY EVERY HUMAN ON THIS PLANET. THIS GHOST HAUNTS SO CONVINCINGLY THAT MOST PEOPLE DON'T EVEN THINK OF IT AS A GHOST; THEY THINK OF IT AS A REAL ENTITY.

THIS GHOST IS SO CONVINCING THAT MOST PEOPLE CAN HARDLY ENVISION A WORLD WITHOUT ITS HAUNTING PRESENCE.

EVEN MANY SUPPOSEDLY RATIONAL, SCIENTIFIC PEOPLE--PEOPLE WHO TEND TO PRIDE THEMSELVES ON THEIR DISBELIEF IN SUCH METAPHYSICAL CONCEPTS AS GHOSTS--NONETHELESS BLINDLY BELIEVE IN THE GHOST OF THIS STORY.

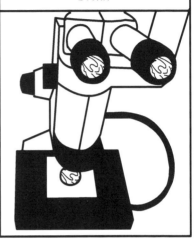

AND WHY WOULDN'T THEY? THIS GHOST ACTUALLY USES ITS SPECIAL POWERS TO GATHER FUNDS USED FOR A SIZABLE AMOUNT OF THE SCIENTIFIC RESEARCH IN THIS WORLD.

EUREKA! I JUST FIGURED OUT HOW TO CONTINUE OUR RESEARCH GRANT FUNDING!

MOST BUSINESS PEOPLE ALSO BELIEVE IN THIS GHOST. GETTING ON THE GOOD SIDE OF THIS GHOST IS GOOD FOR BUSINESS. AND THIS GHOST CAN USE ITS SPECIAL POWERS TO TURN BUSINESSES THEMSELVES INTO GHOSTS. THIS BIT OF MAGIC IS CALLED INCORPORATION.

2

MOST RELIGIOUS PEOPLE BELIEVE IN THIS UNHOLY GHOST.

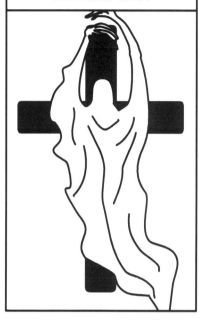

POOR PEOPLE, RICH PEOPLE, SMART PEOPLE, DUMB PEOPLE, SHORT PEOPLE, TALL PEOPLE, VIRTUOUS PEOPLE, CORRUPT PEOPLE, PEOPLE OF EVERY KIND, AND PEOPLE FROM EVERY CORNER OF THE WORLD BELIEVE IN THIS GHOST.

THERE ARE EVEN PEOPLE WHO DRESS UP IN SPECIAL UNIFORMS TO KILL AND DIE FOR THIS GHOST.

PEOPLE POSSESSED BY THIS GHOST DIRECTLY KILLED OVER 200 MILLION PEOPLE IN THE 20TH CENTURY ALONE. AND THAT'S PROBABLY A CONSERVATIVE ESTIMATE.

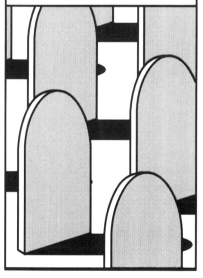

THIS GHOST ROBS PEOPLE, KIDNAPS PEOPLE, AND GENERALLY ENSLAVES PEOPLE ALL OVER THE WORLD IN THE NAME OF PROTECTING IRONIC CONCEPTS OF FREEDOM AND SAFETY.

PROTECTING AND SERVING THE CRAP OUT OF YOU

YET, PEOPLE STILL CHANNEL THIS GHOST TO SUPPOSEDLY PROTECT THEM FROM ALL THE EVILS OF THE WORLD. AND WHEN PEOPLE WANT TO DO GOOD IN THE WORLD, THEY DELUSIONALLY TURN TO THIS SAME GHOST TO FACILITATE THAT SUPPOSED GOOD.

HOW DARE YOU RESIST? THIS IS FOR CHARITY DAMNIT!

MADNESS I TELL YOU! PEOPLE OFTEN EVEN GET SENTIMENTALLY TEARY EYED WHEN CONFRONTED WITH SYMBOLS OF THIS GHOST; LIKE IN THE FORM OF SHEETS OF NYLON AND WAR ANTHEMS. SUCH ROBOTIC BEHAVIOR IS A SURE SIGN OF POSSESSION.

GET THE POINT? UNLESS YOU ARE REALLY DENSE, YOU, OF COURSE, ALREADY KNOW THAT THE GHOST I'M TALKING ABOUT IS GOVERNMENT.

THE GOVERNMENT IS THE GHOST; IT'S A PHANTOM. THERE IS NO SUCH THING AS GOVERNMENT OUTSIDE OF THE HUMAN MIND. GOVERNMENT IS JUST A COLLECTIVE DELUSION.

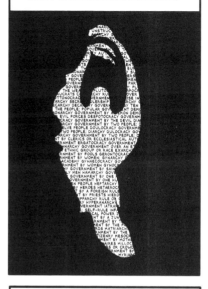

BUT MOST PEOPLE ARE SO HAUNTED BY THE GHOST OF GOVERNMENT THAT THE IDEA OF NO GOVERNMENT IS NEVER EVEN CONSIDERED... EXCEPT AS A FORM OF APOCALYPTIC DISASTER.

HOWEVER, THE FACT IS THAT PEOPLE ALREADY LIVE IN A WORLD WITHOUT GOVERNMENT.

GOVERNMENT IS JUST A DELUSION TO BEGIN WITH, SO IT DOESN'T REALLY EXIST. BUT MOREOVER, MOST PEOPLE LIVE MOST OF THEIR LIVES WITHOUT HAVING ANYTHING TO DO WITH GOVERNMENT ANYWAY.

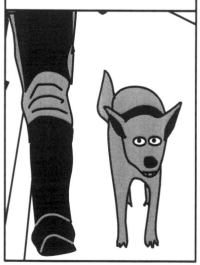

5

THE WAY PEOPLE SPEND MOST OF THEIR LIVES IS IN A STATE OF PEACEFUL, VOLUNTARY INTERACTION WITH OTHER HUMANS...AND THUS NO NEED FOR GOVERNMENT. IN OTHER WORDS, PEOPLE DEFAULT TO A STATE OF **VOLUNTARYISM** IN THE ABSENCE OF GOVERNMENT.

EXAMPLE 1: IT IS NOT ILLEGAL TO CUT IN LINE, YET PEOPLE RARELY DO IT. PEOPLE KNOW THAT TO DO SO WOULD MEAN BEING OSTRACIZED.

EXAMPLE 2: LEAVING A TIP FOR A WAITER ISN'T REQUIRED BY LAW, BUT MOST PEOPLE DO IT ANYWAY BECAUSE IT IS CUSTOMARY AND PEOPLE NATURALLY LIKE TO REWARD WHAT THEY VALUE.

VOLUNTARYISM IS NOTHING BUT SIMPLE, MORAL LOGIC. VOLUNTARYISM IS THE SIMPLE, MORAL, LOGICAL STANCE THAT ALL FORMS OF HUMAN ASSOCIATION SHOULD BE VOLUNTARY...AND THUS FREE OF FORCE AND AGGRESSION.

MR. VOLUNTARY

THEREFORE, TO DISAGREE WITH VOLUNTARYISM IS TO SUPPORT THE USE OF FORCE IN THE REALM OF HUMAN ASSOCIATION.

ANY PERSON WHO SUPPORTS THE USE OF FORCE IN THE REALM OF HUMAN ASSOCIATION IS SIMPLY A FOOL AT BEST AND A TYRANT AT WORST.

EITHER WAY, SUCH A PERSON, BY SUPPORTING FORCE, INEVITABLY SETS UP THE CONDITIONS FOR BEING ON THE RECEIVING END OF FORCE. AND TO BE ON THE RECEIVING END OF FORCE IS TO BE ENSLAVED AT BEST AND DEAD AT WORST.

THE GOLDEN RULE

DO UNTO OTHERS AS YOU WOULD HAVE THEM DO UNTO YOU.

THE GOLDEN RULE OF VOLUNTARYISM

DO NOT INITIATE FORCE ON OTHERS IF YOU WOULD NOT HAVE THEM INITIATE FORCE ON YOU.

AFTER ALL, DO YOU KNOW WHAT THE SIMPLEST REASON WHY YOU SHOULDN'T GO AROUND ASSAULTING OR KILLING PEOPLE IS?

WELL, IT IS BECAUSE EVENTUALLY SOMEONE IS GOING TO FIGHT BACK AND BEAT YOU TO A PULP...OR JUST OUTRIGHT KILL YOU IN SELF-DEFENSE. THAT FACT REQUIRES NO PRE-ESTABLISHED MORAL VIRTUE. WHAT YOU DO TO OTHERS, THEY ARE EVENTUALLY GOING TO DO TO YOU.

THE ACCEPTANCE OF FORCE IN HUMAN ASSOCIATION SETS UP AN INSANE LOOP; IT IS A GAME OF SLAVES AND MASTERS: VICTIMS AND VICTIMIZERS.

7

THE SAD TRUTH IS THAT MOST PEOPLE WALKING THE FACE OF THE EARTH TODAY, BY DEFAULT, ARE STUCK IN THE SLAVES AND MASTERS GAME OF FORCE.

THAT IS BECAUSE TO SUPPORT AND THUS VALIDATE, IN ANY WAY, THE UBIQUITOUS, YET FICTITIOUS, MONOPOLY ON THE INITIATION OF FORCE KNOWN AS GOVERNMENT IS TO PERPETUATE THE SLAVES AND MASTERS GAME.

I MEAN, IF YOU WANT TO KNOW WHAT THE ANTITHESIS OF VOLUNTARYISM LOOKS LIKE, YOU NEED NOT LOOK MUCH FURTHER THAN GOVERNMENT.

A VOLUNTARYIST MINDED MAN BY THE NAME OF **HENRY DAVID THOREAU** MADE THE ACUTE OBSERVATION IN HIS FAMOUS ESSAY ON CIVIL DISOBEDIENCE THAT:

GOVERNMENT IS BEST WHICH GOVERNS NOT AT ALL; AND WHEN MEN ARE PREPARED FOR IT, THAT WILL BE THE KIND OF GOVERNMENT WHICH THEY WILL HAVE.

8

CONTRARY TO POPULAR DELUSION, GOVERNMENT IS BY NO MEANS A KEYSTONE OF CIVILIZATION. GOVERNMENT IS MERELY A PRIMITIVE TOOL IN THE TOOLBOX OF PRIMITIVE SOCIETY.

VOLUNTARYISM IS WHAT WILL REPLACE THAT PRIMITIVE TOOL WHEN, AS THOREAU PUT IT: MEN ARE PREPARED FOR IT. AND THIS BOOK IS PART OF THAT PREPARATION.

VOLUNTARYISM IS VERY SIMPLE AND INTUITIVE, BUT MOST PEOPLE HAVE NEVER HEARD OF IT...WHICH IS A TESTAMENT TO THE DEPTH OF GOVERNMENT PROPAGANDA.

THE MERE MENTION OF A STATELESS SOCIETY EVOKES STRAW MAN DISMISSALS OF THE CONCEPT BY CITING PLACES LIKE SOMALIA AS THE KIND OF HELL THAT RESULTS FROM A STATELESS SOCIETY.

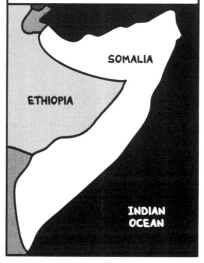

THE REALITY IS THAT SOMALIAN STATELESSNESS WASN'T THE RESULT OF A PHILOSOPHICAL REVOLUTION OF VOLUNTARYISM BUT INSTEAD WAS THE RESULT OF THE EPIC FAILURE OF GOVERNMENT IN THE FIRST PLACE.

BURNING DOWN CHURCHES DOESN'T MAKE PEOPLE TURN INTO ATHEISTS. AND THE SAME APPLIES TO BURNING DOWN GOVERNMENT.[1]

THE SAME CULTURAL PROGRAMMING THAT RUNS A REGION WITH A GOVERNMENT IS THE SAME CULTURAL PROGRAMMING THAT RUNS A REGION AFTER A GOVERNMENT.

PEOPLE MUST REALIZE THAT THERE IS NO POINT IN TRYING TO CHANGE THE WORLD. TO TRY TO CHANGE THE WORLD IS PART OF THE SLAVES AND MASTERS GAME OF FORCE.

THE WORLD IS AN EFFECT OF THE THINKING OF THE PEOPLE WHO MAKE UP THE WORLD. THEREFORE, THINKING IS THE CAUSE OF THE WORLD. CHANGE THE THINKING AND CHANGE THE WORLD.

VOLUNTARYISM OFFERS A DIFFERENT WAY OF THINKING; IT IS A SIMPLE, LOGICAL FORMULA FOR CALCULATING THE PARAMETERS OF SANE, MORAL HUMAN INTERACTION.

THE IMPLEMENTATION OF VOLUNTARYISM REVOLVES AROUND A MAIN PRINCIPLE, WHICH WE WILL EXPLORE IN THIS BOOK. THAT PRINCIPLE IS **NON-AGGRESSION**.

THE NON-AGGRESSION PRINCIPLE IS A FORMULA FOR MAXIMAL FREEDOM AND PEACE IN HUMAN ASSOCIATION.

NON-AGGRESSION PRINCIPLE: AGGRESSION IS INHERENTLY ILLEGITIMATE. AGGRESSION IS THE INITIATION OR THREAT OF VIOLENCE AGAINST A PERSON, OR A PERSON'S PROPERTY. ANY UNSOLICITED ACTIONS OF OTHERS THAT PHYSICALLY AFFECT AN INDIVIDUAL'S PROPERTY, INCLUDING THAT PERSON'S BODY, NO MATTER IF THE RESULT OF THOSE ACTIONS IS DAMAGING, BENEFICIAL, OR NEUTRAL TO THE OWNER, ARE CONSIDERED VIOLENT WHEN THEY ARE AGAINST THE OWNER'S WILL AND INTERFERE WITH HIS RIGHT TO SELF-DETERMINATION, AS BASED ON THE PRINCIPLE OF SELF-OWNERSHIP.

THIS IS NOT A UTOPIAN BOOK. REMOVING INSTITUTIONALIZED FORCE IN THE WORLD IN FAVOR OF PURE VOLUNTARYISM WOULD NOT COMPLETELY ELIMINATE FORCE IN THE WORLD. HOWEVER, IT WOULD CREATE THE NECESSARY POSITIVE FEEDBACK MECHANISMS TO DRASTICALLY REDUCE FORCE, WHILE AT THE SAME TIME INCREASING PROSPERITY, EFFICIENCY, AND OVERALL PEACE.

VOLUNTARILY NEGOTIATE

EVERYONE WINS　　　　**AGREE**

IN THE CURRENT GOVERNMENT-DOMINATED SOCIAL SYSTEM, THE SO-CALLED CONTROL OF FORCE IS LOCKED IN A SELF-CONTRADICTING TAUTOLOGY THAT SAYS:

SOME PEOPLE ARE BAD SO WE NEED PEOPLE, OF WHICH SOME ARE BAD, TO HAVE A MONOPOLY ON FORCE TO PROTECT US FROM SOME PEOPLE WHO ARE BAD, BECAUSE SOME PEOPLE ARE BAD SO WE NEED PEOPLE, OF WHICH SOME ARE BAD, TO HAVE A MONOPOLY ON FORCE TO PROTECT US FROM SOME PEOPLE...

SO, IT DOESN'T TAKE A GENIUS TO RECOGNIZE THE LOGICAL ABSURDITY OF STATE FORCE.

I'M GOING TO HAVE YOU WATCH THE HEN HOUSE.

SOUNDS GREAT TO ME!

BUT DENIAL IS RAMPANT IN THE FACE OF SUCH TRUTHS FOR THOSE ENTRENCHED IN A LIFE SCULPTED BY STATE **PROPAGANDA**.

ARE YOU YOURSELF SUCH A CONFUSED AND BLINDED SLAVE?

I'M NOT A SLAVE, I'M JUST REALISTIC.

MY SHACKLES KEEP ME SAFE.

LET'S TEST AND SEE. IF I WERE TO TELL YOU THAT GOVERNMENT IS A LOGICALLY IMMORAL FORCE THAT IS COMPLETELY UNNECESSARY FOR AND ACTUALLY DETRIMENTAL TO HAVING A HEALTHY, VIRTUOUS, PROSPEROUS SOCIETY, WHAT WOULD YOUR KNEE-JERK DEFENSES OF THE STATE BE?

WELL, SINCE SUCH DEFENSES ARE QUITE PREDICTABLE, I'LL LIST A SAMPLING OF SOME VERY COMMON ONES.

WHO WILL MAKE AND MAINTAIN THE ROADS?

WHO WILL EDUCATE ALL THE CHILDREN?

WHO WILL KEEP THE VOID OF NO GOVERNMENT FROM BEING FILLED BY AN EVEN WORSE GOVERNMENT?

WHO WILL STOP MONOPOLIES?

YOU MEAN MONOPOLIES LIKE THE GOVERNMENT?

WHO WILL STOP THIEVES, RAPISTS, AND MURDERS?

WHO WILL STOP CORPORATIONS FROM POLLUTING?

WE WILL ADDRESS THESE DELUSIONAL CONCERNS IN DETAIL THROUGHOUT THE BOOK. FOR NOW, JUST REALIZE THAT SUCH QUESTIONS REALLY MAKE LITTLE MORE SENSE THAN ASKING:

WHO WILL MAKE CELL PHONES?

WHO WILL MAKE FASHIONABLE SHOES?

WHO WILL MAKE DINNER?

THE ANSWER IS THAT PEOPLE WILL BECAUSE THAT IS WHAT PEOPLE WANT.

AS WE CLOSE OUT THIS INTRODUCTORY CHAPTER, I WANT TO SHARE WITH YOU A ZEN STORY ABOUT A MONK.[2]

IN THIS STORY, A MONK WAS NOT ABLE TO FREE HIS MIND USING NORMAL ZEN METHODS. THEREFORE, THE MONK'S TEACHER TOLD HIM TO:

THINK OF NOTHING BUT AN OX.

14

DAY AFTER DAY, THE MONK THOUGHT OF AN OX... MEDITATED ON AN OX.

EVENTUALLY, THE TEACHER CAME TO THE MONK'S CELL AND SAID:

COME OUT HERE --I WANT TO TALK TO YOU.

THE MONK SAID:

I CAN'T GET OUT, MY HORNS WON'T FIT THROUGH THE DOOR.

WITH THAT INSIGHT, THE MONK'S MIND WAS FINALLY FREED. HUMANS SUBJECTED TO A LIFETIME OF PROPAGANDA ABOUT THE NECESSITY OF GOVERNMENT ARE JUST LIKE THE MONK TRAPPED BY IMAGINARY HORNS.

COME ON! IT'S TIME TO GET RID OF THOSE IMAGINARY HORNS.

CHAPTER ONE

SLAVES AND MASTERS

THE GHOST KNOWN AS GOVERNMENT IS THE ULTIMATE SLAVE MASTER. GOVERNMENT HAUNTS MOST PEOPLE INTO A FORM OF BLIND, SUBSERVIENT SLAVERY.

SUCH SLAVERY IS OFTEN THOUGHT OF BY THE SLAVES AS THE PRICE OF FREEDOM. AS IF THAT MAKES ANY SENSE.

PRICE: SLAVERY

THERE ARE FIVE UNIVERSAL TRAITS OF THE ENSLAVED:

1. THEY DON'T CONTROL THE MEANS OF PRODUCTION.

2. THEY DON'T HAVE ANY REAL POLITICAL INFLUENCE.

3. THEY ARE HEAVILY TAXED. (IF SLAVES PAY 100% TAX, AT WHAT POINT IS IT NOT SLAVERY?)

4. THEY ARE INDEBTED AND THUS INDENTURED.

5. THEY ARE SYSTEMICALLY ABUSED. [6]

THE MORE ENSLAVED YOU ARE, THE MORE THOSE TRAITS APPLY TO YOU.

THE GOVERNMENT SLAVE SYSTEM MAKES FOR A KIND OF PYRAMID RANGING FROM TOTAL SLAVES AT THE BOTTOM TO TOTAL MASTERS AT THE TOP.

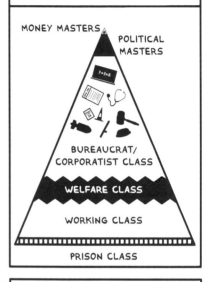

MONEY MASTERS

POLITICAL MASTERS

BUREAUCRAT/ CORPORATIST CLASS

WELFARE CLASS

WORKING CLASS

PRISON CLASS

THE MASTERS ARE PEOPLE WHO USE THE GHOST OF GOVERNMENT TO EXTRACT WEALTH FROM THE SLAVES. IT SETS UP A **CORPORATIST** SYSTEM.

CORPORATISM:

1. THE MERGER OF STATE AND CORPORATE POWER.

2. THE INFLUENCE OF BUSINESS CORPORATIONS IN POLITICS.

3. THE USE OF THE GUNS OF GOVERNMENT TO EXTRACT WEALTH USING VARIOUS FORMS OF STATE FACILITATED FORCE.

THERE IS A LOT OF ROOM IN-BETWEEN TOTAL SLAVE AND TOTAL MASTER. AND IT IS THAT IN-BETWEEN SPACE THAT KEEPS THE SYSTEM ALIVE. REALISTICALLY, A FEW MASTERS COULDN'T KEEP THE SLAVES IN LINE WITHOUT THE HELP OF THE SLAVES THEMSELVES.

TOTAL SLAVE

TOTAL MASTER

17

AT THE TOP OF THE PYRAMID, YOU FIND PEOPLE WHO CONTROL THE MONETARY SYSTEM. THEY ESSENTIALLY CREATE MONEY OUT OF THIN AIR AND USE IT TO INDEBT THE SLAVES.

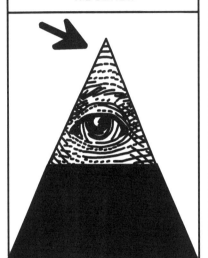

NEXT ARE FEDERAL POLITICIANS, PUNDITS, LOBBYISTS, CERTAIN CELEBRITIES, AND PEOPLE WHO RUN AND OWN MULTI-NATIONAL CORPORATIONS (CORPORATISTS).

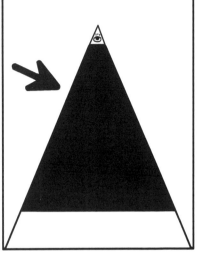

LOWER DOWN, YOU FIND PEOPLE EMPLOYED DIRECTLY BY THE GOVERNMENT, SUCH AS LAW ENFORCEMENT, MILITARY, FIREFIGHTERS, PUBLIC SCHOOL TEACHERS, STATE UNIVERSITY PROFESSORS, POLITICIANS, BUREAUCRATS OF EVERY KIND, ANYONE IN A PUBLIC SECTOR UNION.

AND YOU ALSO FIND PEOPLE WHO MAKE GOOD MONEY EMPLOYED BY BUSINESSES CONNECTED TO THE GOVERNMENT, LIKE THE INDUSTRIAL MILITARY COMPLEX, THE HEALTHCARE INDUSTRIAL COMPLEX, LAWYERS, TAX PROFESSIONALS; THEIR PAYCHECKS AMOUNT TO CORPORATE WELFARE.

NEXT, YOU FIND PEOPLE WHO DIRECTLY RECEIVE WELFARE FROM THE GOVERNMENT. IT'S USUALLY NOT AS LUCRATIVE AS WORKING FOR OR BEING IN BUSINESS WITH THE GOVERNMENT, BUT IT STILL TRANSLATES INTO PROFITING BY WAY OF GOVERNMENT FORCE.

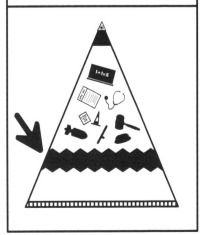

18

NEXT IS THE AVERAGE PERSON. THESE PEOPLE ARE THE PEOPLE WHO GIVE THE GOVERNMENT MORE, IN THE FORM OF TAXATION, THAN THEY EVER RECEIVE BACK IN THE FORM OF THINGS THEY WOULD HAVE ACTUALLY WILLINGLY PAID FOR IN A TOTALLY FREE MARKET ABSENT OF GOVERNMENT.

THEN AT THE VERY BOTTOM ARE PEOPLE LITERALLY IMPRISONED BY THE GOVERNMENT.

WHAT THIS PYRAMID SHOWS IS BASICALLY THE TAXATION HIERARCHY. THE PLANTATIONS KNOWN AS MODERN COUNTRIES ARE SIMPLY TAX FARMS OF FREE-RANGE SLAVES WHERE THE WEALTH OF THE TRULY PRODUCTIVE CLASS IS SIPHONED BY A MASTER CLASS.

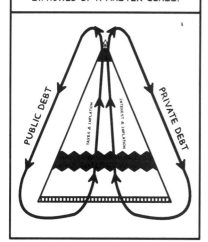

THIS IS DONE THROUGH VARIOUS FORMS OF TAXATION. TAXATION IS A SUBTLE FORM OF THE INITIATION OF FORCE. IT'S SUBTLE IN AS LONG AS A PERSON ACTUALLY PAYS WHATEVER TAXES ARE DUE.

19

WHEN PEOPLE DON'T COMPLY, IT BECOMES LESS SUBTLE AND INEVITABLY LEADS TO A FORCEFUL KIDNAPPING AND IMPRISONMENT OF SOME KIND.

GIVE US 33% OF YOUR MONEY AND NO ONE GETS HURT!

IN THAT SENSE, TAXATION IS QUITE SIMPLY THEFT. AND IF YOU WANT TO DISAGREE WITH THAT ASSESSMENT, THEN TO HONOR YOUR OWN FORM OF LOGIC I GUESS IT WOULD BE PERFECTLY FINE FOR ME TO DEMAND YOU GIVE ME HALF YOUR MONEY OR I'LL LOCK YOU IN A CAGE. WHAT? YOU DIDN'T KNOW? IT'S PART OF THE SOCIAL CONTRACT I MADE WITH YOU WITHOUT YOUR CONSENT.

THERE IS REALLY NO VOLUNTARY FORM OF TAXATION ANYMORE THAN THERE IS SUCH A THING AS CONSENSUAL RAPE. ANYTHING THAT IS TAXED IS A LIMITATION ON FREE, VOLUNTARY HUMAN INTERACTION.

CITIZENS OF COUNTRIES ARE'NT GIVEN THE OPTION OF SIGNING AN INDIVIDUAL CONTRACT GIVING THEM A CHOICE TO PAY TAXES OR NOT. AT BEST, PEOPLE ARE ONLY GIVEN THE CHOICE TO MOVE TO A DIFFERENT TAX FARM, WHICH IS NOT MUCH OF A CHOICE.

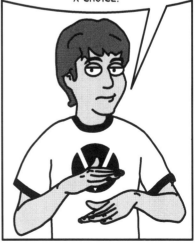

PEOPLE ARE TOLD THAT THEY CAN CAST A LITTLE VOTE EVERY NOW AND THEN TO TRY TO CHANGE THE TAXES. BUT THAT'S A LOSING EFFORT AND MOSTLY JUST A WASTE OF TIME.

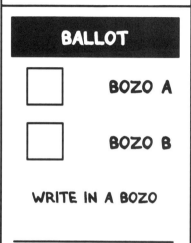

DEMOCRACY IS ACTUALLY QUITE DUMB, BECAUSE A MOB DOESN'T HAVE ALL THE ANSWERS. OFTEN, THE SOFTEST VOICE HAS THE BIGGEST SOLUTIONS. AND A DEMOCRATIC REPUBLIC DOESN'T FIX THE DEFICIENCIES OF DEMOCRACY EITHER.

IF I WANT TO BE A PLUMBER, I DON'T HAVE TO APPEAL TO A MAJORITY VOTE OF OTHERS TO BECOME A PLUMBER. SO, WHY SHOULD I HAVE TO APPEAL TO A MAJORITY VOTE TO DO WHAT I WISH WITH ALL THE FRUITS OF MY LABORS AS A PLUMBER?

POLITICAL ACTION IS THUS EXTREMELY INEFFICIENT AND THE SUPPORT OF A COERCIVE SYSTEM.

IF A GIVEN DEMOCRACY IS TRUE AND VALID AND INDEED REFLECTS THE ACCEPTED WILL OF THE PEOPLE, THEN THE SAME STUFF WOULD GO ON IN A FREE SOCIETY WITHOUT GOVERNMENT.

AND IF DEMOCRACY DOESN'T INDEED REFLECT THE ACCEPTED WILL OF THE PEOPLE, THEN IT IS A LIE AND THUS THE GOVERNMENT IS A LIE. SO, EITHER WAY, VOTING IS A FARCE AND GOVERNMENT IS A DETRIMENT.

BUT WHAT IS AN EVEN BIGGER FARCE IS THAT SIMPLY BEING BORN ON MOST PLOTS OF LAND ON THIS PLANET OBLIGATES A PERSON INTO BEING OWNED BY A GOVERNMENT.

IMAGINARY TAX-FARM BORDER

GOVERNMENTS, IN GENERAL, DON'T ALLOW PEOPLE TO ACTUALLY OWN THEIR OWN LAND BUT INSTEAD FORCE PEOPLE TO RENT IT IN THE FORM OF PROPERTY TAXES OF SOME KIND.

HOME FOR SALE

BY RENTER/OWNER

THEREFORE, ALMOST ALL LAND IN THIS WORLD IS HAUNTED BY THE GHOST OF GOVERNMENT. YOU MAY THINK YOU OWN A HOME ON A NICE PLOT OF LAND WITH THE MORTGAGE ALL PAID OFF, BUT, IN MOST CIRCUMSTANCES, THE GOVERNMENT HAUNTS YOUR HOUSE AND WILL DRIVE YOU OUT LIKE A **POLTERGEIST** IF YOU DON'T GIVE UP WHATEVER PORTION OF THE FRUITS OF YOUR LABORS IT ASKS.

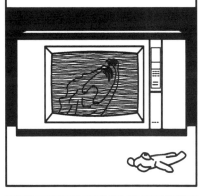

THE RIGHT TO PRIVATE PROPERTY IS ESSENTIAL TO A FREE SOCIETY. ARGUING AGAINST THE RIGHT TO PRIVATE PROPERTY EVENTUALLY LEADS TO THE IDEA THAT PEOPLE SHOULDN'T HAVE THE RIGHT TO OWN THEIR OWN BODIES.

AND THAT IS PRECISELY THE KIND OF THINKING THAT THE GOVERNMENT EXPLOITS. THAT KIND OF THINKING NOT ONLY LEADS TO THINGS LIKE THE JUSTIFICATION OF TAXATION, BUT IT ALSO LEADS TO THE JUSTIFICATION OF THINGS LIKE SENDING PEOPLE OFF TO DIE IN WARS, RESTRICTING WHAT SUBSTANCES PEOPLE CAN PUT IN THEIR BODIES, AND TO POLLUTION.

YEP, YOU HEARD ME RIGHT, POLLUTION. GOVERNMENT MAKES POLLUTION POSSIBLE SINCE POLLUTION REPRESENTS A LACK OF PROTECTION AND CONTAINMENT OF PRIVATE PROPERTY. BUT WE'LL DELVE MORE INTO THAT SUBJECT LATER.

THE AVERAGE SLAVE MAY NOT LIKE TAXATION, BUT THE AVERAGE SLAVE HAS NONETHELESS BEEN CONDITIONED INTO ACCEPTING IT AS A NECESSARY PART OF FUNDING GOVERNMENT. BECAUSE THE AVERAGE SLAVE CAN'T IMAGINE THAT THERE IS ANOTHER CHOICE BUT TO HAVE A GOVERNMENT.

AT BEST, MOST SLAVES WILL GO AS FAR AS TO SAY WE NEED A SMALL, MINIMAL GOVERNMENT INSTEAD OF A BIG ONE. BUT THAT IS A FANTASY, BECAUSE THE EXPERIMENT OF THE UNITED STATES IS A CASE IN POINT THAT SHOWS THAT SMALL GOVERNMENT ONLY LEADS TO MASSIVE GOVERNMENT.

A SMALLER GUN IS STILL A LETHAL WEAPON

THE WEALTH CREATED BY A VERY FREE COUNTRY IS SO GREAT THAT THE GOVERNMENT AUTOMATICALLY GROWS IN ORDER TO SIPHON THAT WEALTH TO THE MASTERS.

THAT'S WHY SMALL GOVERNMENT PEOPLE, LIKE LIBERTARIANS, JUST NEED TO GIVE IT UP ALREADY AND BECOME PURE VOLUNTARYISTS. A MUCH BETTER STARTING BID FOR NEGOTIATING DOWN THE SIZE OF GOVERNMENT IS TO START WITH A BID OF ZERO.

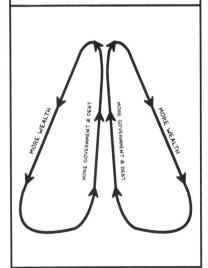

THE MOST REALISTIC WAY A GOVERNMENT COULD THEORETICALLY STAY SMALL IS IF ITS GROWTH WAS CONSTANTLY THREATENED BY A REVOLUTION OF DOING AWAY WITH IT ALTOGETHER.

THE REALITY IS THAT A LITTLE BIT OF INSTITUTIONALIZED INITIATION OF FORCE IS STILL TOO MUCH. EITHER THE INITIATION OF FORCE IS WRONG AND IMMORAL, OR IT ISN'T.

EITHER

OR

AND IF IT ISN'T, THEN WHOEVER SAID THAT SHOULD BE CLUBBED ALONGSIDE THE HEAD FOR THE SAKE OF LOGICAL CONSISTENCY.

FORCE IS NECESSARY, DUH.

POLICE STATE

IF YOU SAY SO.

ONE WAY YOU CAN VERY EASILY REALIZE THAT VOLUNTARYISM IS A COMPLETELY CORRECT AND MORAL STANCE IS THE FACT THAT BY TAKING THE STANCE OF VOLUNTARYISM YOU CAN WIN ANY POLITICAL ARGUMENT.

FOR EXAMPLE, SAY SOMEONE TELLS ME I'M AN IDIOT TO THINK THAT A COMPLETELY FREE SOCIETY WOULD WORK BETTER THAN GOVERNMENT BECAUSE:

GOVERNMENT MAKES THINGS LIKE PUBLIC EDUCATION POSSIBLE AND WITHOUT PUBLIC EDUCATION POOR KIDS WOULD BE DUMB.

WELL, THAT ISN'T MUCH OF AN ARGUMENT, BECAUSE I'M STILL WAITING TO SEE ALL THESE AMAZINGLY SMART POOR KIDS PRODUCED BY GOVERNMENT EDUCATION. PLUS, THE MERE FACT THAT PEOPLE CARE ABOUT EDUCATING POOR KIDS IS CASE IN POINT THAT IT WOULD BE TAKEN CARE OF IN A FREE SOCIETY.

BUT THAT ISN'T EVEN RELEVANT AS TO WHY I AS A VOLUNTARYIST AM GUARANTEED TO WIN THIS ARGUMENT.

TO WIN THIS ARGUMENT, ALL I'D HAVE TO SAY TO SUCH A PERSON IS:

DO YOU SUPPORT THE INITIATION OF VIOLENCE AGAINST ME FOR SIMPLY DISAGREEING WITH YOU? [1]

26

BECAUSE IF I REFUSE TO PAY TAXES TO PAY FOR THINGS LIKE PUBLIC SCHOOLING, GOVERNMENT THUGS ARE EVENTUALLY GOING TO COME AROUND AND USE VIOLENCE AGAINST ME FOR NOT BEING AN OBEDIENT TAX SLAVE.

IF THE PERSON SAYS:

YES, I DO SUPPORT THE INITIATION OF VIOLENCE AGAINST YOU FOR DISAGREEING.

THEN SIMPLY SAY SOMETHING LIKE:

WELL, SINCE I DISAGREE WITH YOU, FOLLOWING YOUR OWN INGENIOUS LOGIC, I GUESS IT WOULD BE PERFECTLY REASONABLE FOR ME TO PULL OUT A BLUNT OBJECT RIGHT NOW AND BEAT IT AGAINST YOUR HEAD UNTIL I HEAR THAT LITTLE PEA ROLLING AROUND IN YOUR CRANIUM.

OBVIOUSLY, MOST SANE PEOPLE WOULD HAVE A LITTLE EUREKA MOMENT AND SAY:

NO, I DON'T SUPPORT THE INITIATION OF VIOLENCE AGAINST YOU FOR DISAGREEING WITH ME. DAMN, YOU GOT ME. I SEE WHAT YOU MEAN.

THE PERSON WILL STILL PROBABLY TRY TO SAY:

BUT, BUT, BUT, BUT, BUT.

BUT NOTHING. THE WORLD DOESN'T NEED CHARITY AT THE END OF A GUN. THAT'S NOT CHARITY. THAT'S A CRIMINAL WEALTH EXTRACTION SCHEME.

TAXATION COMES IN MANY FORMS. THINGS LIKE LICENSING AND PERMITTING ARE FORMS OF TAXATION, BUT SO ARE THINGS LIKE PUBLIC DEBT AND INFLATION.

ACCOUNTS RECEIVABLE TAX
AVIATION FUEL TAX
BUILDING PERMIT TAX
CAPITAL GAINS TAX
CDL LICENSE TAX
CIGARETTE TAX
CORPORATE INCOME TAX
COURT FINES
DOG LICENSE TAX
FEDERAL INCOME TAX
FEDERAL UNEMPLOYMENT TAX
FISHING LICENSE TAX
FOOD LICENSE TAX
FUEL PERMIT TAX
GASOLINE TAX
HUNTING LICENSE TAX
INHERITANCE TAX
INVENTORY TAX
IRS INTEREST CHARGES
IRS PENALTIES
LIQUOR TAX
LOCAL INCOME TAX
LUXURY TAXES
MARRIAGE LICENSE TAX
MEDICARE TAX
PROPERTY TAX
REAL ESTATE TAX
SERVICE CHARGE TAXES
SOCIAL SECURITY TAX
ROAD USAGE TAXES
SALES TAXES
RECREATIONAL VEHICLE TAX
ROAD TOLL BOOTH TAXES
SCHOOL TAX

WHENEVER YOU BUY ANYTHING, YOU DON'T JUST PAY A SALES TAX, YOU ALSO PAY ALL THE TAXES (LICENSES, REGULATION COMPLIANCE, DEBT) THAT WENT INTO MAKING THAT PRODUCT.

STATE INCOME TAX
STATE UNEMPLOYMENT TAX
TELEPHONE FEDERAL EXCISE TAX
TELEPHONE FEDERAL UNIVERSAL SERVICE FEE TAX
TELEPHONE FEDERAL, STATE AND LOCAL SURCHARGE TAXES
TELEPHONE MINIMUM USAGE SURCHARGE TAX
TELEPHONE RECURRING AND NON-RECURRING CHARGES TAX
TELEPHONE STATE AND LOCAL TAX
TELEPHONE USAGE CHARGE TAX
TOLL BRIDGE/TUNNEL TAXES
TOURIST TAXES
TRAFFIC FINES
TRAILER REGISTRATION TAX
UTILITY TAXES
VEHICLE LICENSE REGISTRATION TAX
VEHICLE SALES TAX
WATERCRAFT REGISTRATION TAX
WELL PERMIT TAX
WORKERS COMPENSATION TAX

FOR THAT REASON, IT IS DIFFICULT TO TAX THE RICH. THE RICH TEND TO BE RICH BECAUSE THEY HAVE PRICING POWER. THEY CAN RAISE PRICES TO MAKE UP FOR TAXES.*

28

* TO THE EXTENT THE MARKET WILL TOLERATE

BEYOND TAXES, DEBT IS ONE OF THE DIRTIEST TRICKS OF GOVERNMENT. BECAUSE DEBT IS AN ATTEMPT TO PASS ON THE COST OF PRESENT GOVERNMENT TO THOSE WHO HAVE NO SAY WHATSOEVER IN THE MATTER: CHILDREN AND FUTURE GENERATIONS.

THEREFORE, GOVERNMENT DEBT IS INSTITUTIONALIZED CHILD ABUSE.

WHY DO YOU HATE ME?

GOVERNMENT DEBT IS USUALLY ONLY EVER REALLY PAID OFF THROUGH INFLATION. GOVERNMENT DEBT HAS HISTORICALLY ALWAYS LED TO THE DEVALUATION OF THE CURRENCY IN WHICH THE DEBT WAS ISSUED.

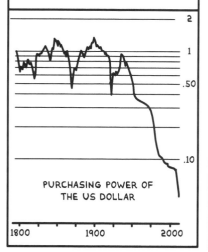

PURCHASING POWER OF THE US DOLLAR

THE SYMPTOM OF INFLATION IS RISING PRICES. INFLATION IS THE RESULT OF THE MISMANAGEMENT OF A CURRENCY.

I JUST DON'T FEEL LIKE I HAVE ANY REAL VALUE.

29

WHEN CURRENCY SUPPLY AND INTEREST RATES ARE OUT OF TUNE WITH ECONOMIC GROWTH OR EQUILIBRIUM, WHICH ALMOST ALWAYS OCCURS IN A CENTRALLY MANIPULATED ECONOMY, THEN THE PURCHASING POWER OF A GIVEN CURRENCY IS DESTABILIZED.

DESTABILIZATION CAN ALSO MEAN DEFLATION, WHICH LEADS TO FALLING PRICES. BUT THE BIAS OF GOVERNMENTS IS ALMOST ALWAYS TO INFLATE, BECAUSE IT MAKES PAST DEBTS WORTH LESS.

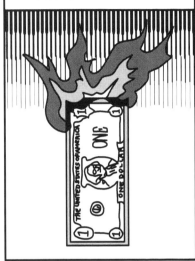

THAT'S WHY THINGS PRETTY MUCH ALWAYS GET MORE EXPENSIVE. THE ONLY THING THAT TENDS TO DRIVE DOWN PRICES IS TECHNOLOGY AND COMPETITION.

THE TELLTALE SIGN OF THE REAL VALUE OF A CURRENCY IS THE CURRENCY'S VALUE RELATIVE TO FINITE RESOURCES, PARTICULARLY GOLD AND SILVER.

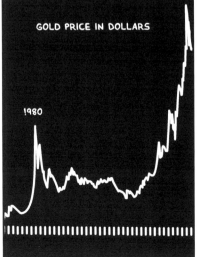

GOLD PRICE IN DOLLARS

1980

GOLD AND SILVER ARE ACTUAL MONEY, NOT CURRENCY. MONEY IS SOMETHING THAT ACTUALLY HOLDS ITS VALUE DUE TO ITS SCARCITY, WHILE CURRENCY IS USUALLY JUST A KIND OF FRAUD IMPLEMENTED OR FACILITATED BY GOVERNMENTS.

THE GROWTH OF GOVERNMENT INEVITABLY LEADS TO THE PROGRESSIVE ABANDONMENT OF COMMODITY MONEY, LIKE GOLD AND SILVER, IN FAVOR OF CURRENCY.

NOTE: AS WE'LL SEE LATER IN THIS BOOK, CURRENCY CAN BE LEGITIMATE MONEY WHEN IT IS FREE MARKET.

THE TIMES

Mr Nixon acts to save Dollar in move for World currency reforms

Daily Mail

2 AM: DOLLAR IS 'DEVALUED'

The Daily Telegra

US HALTS DOLLAR GOLD CONVERSION

Nixon orders wage and price freeze

IN THE CONTEMPORARY WORLD, ALMOST ALL CURRENCIES ARE SIMPLY A FORM OF I-O-U: DEBT. CURRENCY IN THE MODERN WORLD COMES INTO EXISTENCE WHEN SOME PERSON OR INSTITUTION TAKES OUT A LOAN AT INTEREST. THAT LOAN CAN COME FROM ANY BANK, ESPECIALLY A CENTRAL BANK LIKE THE FEDERAL RESERVE.

CONVERSELY, MONEY GOES OUT OF EXISTENCE WHEN A LOAN IS REPAID. BUT A LOAN IS REPAID PLUS INTEREST. THEREFORE, TO PAY INTEREST, EVEN MORE LOANS NEED TO BE MADE TO KEEP ENOUGH MONEY IN THE SYSTEM TO PAY OFF INTEREST. THIS GIVES THE SYSTEM AN AUTOMATIC INFLATIONARY BIAS.

HOW CURRENCY IS CREATED

CENTRAL BANKS LEND IMAGINARY CURRENCY TO BANKS.

BANKS LEND THEIR OWN IMAGINARY CURRENCY TO BUSINESSES, INDIVIDUALS, AND GOVERNMENTS.

ALL THIS CURRENCY IS JUST DEBT.

SOME OF THAT DEBT IS PUT INTO THE FORM OF PHYSICAL CURRENCY.

HOW CURRENCY IS DESTROYED

PHYSICAL CURRENCY IS SPENT AND GOES BACK INTO A BANK.

BUSINESSES, INDIVIDUALS, AND GOVERNMENTS PAY CURRENCY PLUS INTEREST BACK TO BANKS.

BANKS PAY CURRENCY PLUS INTEREST BACK TO THE CENTRAL BANK.

SINCE THE ONLY DEBT THAT NEVER REALLY IS PAID OFF IS GOVERNMENT DEBT, GOVERNMENT DEBT REPRESENTS THE BASE CURRENCY SUPPLY OF A COUNTRY. IN THIS SYSTEM, IF GOVERNMENT PAID OFF ITS NATIONAL DEBT, ITS CURRENCY WOULD BECOME VERY SCARCE LEADING TO DEFLATION AND THUS DECLINING PRICES. CURRENCY WOULD GAIN VALUE INSTEAD OF LOSE IT.

PRIVATE DEBT

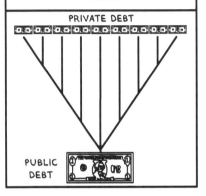

PUBLIC DEBT

THE WHOLE DEBT CURRENCY SCAM FACILITATED BY CONTEMPORARY GOVERNMENTS IS A TRICKY SUBJECT THAT IS BEYOND THE SCOPE OF THIS BOOK. ALL YOU NEED TO REALLY KNOW ABOUT IT IS THAT IT IS A SCAM OF DEBT/TAXATION USED TO SUPPORT THE POWER OF GOVERNMENT AND FUND THOSE IN CAHOOTS WITH GOVERNMENT.

IT IS AN ANTI FREE MARKET SCAM THAT DISTORTS THE WHOLE ECONOMY. THERE IS NO FREE MARKET IF THE MONEY IS NOT FREE MARKET.

IF THE MONEY ISN'T FREE MARKET THERE IS NO FREE MARKET

THEREFORE, ANYONE YOU EVER HEAR TALKING ABOUT THE EXISTENCE OF FREE MARKETS IN THE CONTEMPORARY WORLD IS TOTALLY FULL OF IT. SUCH PEOPLE ARE USUALLY EITHER CLUELESS SLAVES OR JUST TRYING TO GIVE FREE MARKETS A BAD NAME.

THE FREE MARKET WILL DESTROY THE ECONOMY WITHOUT GOVERNMENT REGULATION!

SUPERIMPOSED UPON THE SLAVES AND MASTERS PYRAMID, THE DEBT CURRENCY SYSTEM LOOKS LIKE THIS:

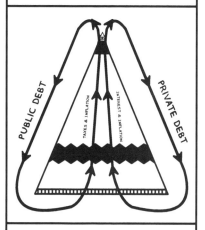

IT CREATES A VORTEX THAT SUCKS THE PRODUCTIVITY OF THE SLAVES UP TO THE MASTERS. [3]

THE GOOD THING ABOUT THIS CURRENCY SCAM IS THAT IT IS INEVITABLY UNSUSTAINABLE AND EVENTUALLY LEADS TO COLLAPSE--DUE TO ITS RELIANCE ON EXPONENTIAL DEBT AND GROWTH TO SUSTAIN ITSELF.

SUCH IS THE NATURE OF THE SLAVE/MASTER DYNAMIC. THE SLAVES LIKE TO ENCOURAGE THE SELF-DESTRUCTIVE HABITS OF THE MASTERS. AND WHETHER CONSCIOUSLY OR UNCONSCIOUSLY, THAT IS WHAT THE SLAVES DO.

WANT SOME MORE FOOD MASTER? YOU'RE STARTING TO LOOK THIN.

BUT INVARIABLY, AFTER THE COLLAPSE, THE SLAVES NEVER THINK TO START OVER WITHOUT A GOVERNMENT, BECAUSE THE COLLAPSE IS ALWAYS BLAMED ON SOME OTHER FACTOR, LIKE THE SO-CALLED FREE MARKET THAT WAS NEVER EVEN REMOTELY FREE. CONSEQUENTLY, THE SLAVES BLINDLY JUST TRY TO RESURRECT THE SCAM AND GET IT RUNNING AGAIN.

IF ONLY THE GOVERNMENT HAD BEEN BIG ENOUGH TO PREVENT THE ECONOMIC COLLAPSE!

IN OTHER WORDS, THE SLAVES DON'T REALLY WANT TO BE FREE; THEY LIKE THE NAIVE VICTIM ROLE AND THE ROLE OF FEEDING THE DESTRUCTION OF THE MASTERS. TIS THE NATURE OF SLAVE MORALITY.

IF I COULDN'T IDENTIFY MYSELF WITH BEING A VICTIM, I'D BE NOBODY?

PEOPLE ALWAYS SAY:

IF ONLY WE COULD ELECT THE RIGHT PEOPLE, GOVERNMENT WOULD BE FINE. MY BRAND OF TYRANNY WOULD WORK AND WOULDN'T BE CORRUPT.

BUT THE NATURE OF GOVERNMENT DOESN'T PROVIDE THE FEEDBACK MECHANISMS FOR GETTING THE SO-CALLED RIGHT PEOPLE INTO OFFICE. NOR DOES THE NATURE OF GOVERNMENT PROVIDE THE FEEDBACK MECHANISMS TO ALLOCATE RESOURCES EFFICIENTLY AND VOLUNTARILY.

DO STUFF THAT'S BENEFICIAL SHORT-TERM AT LONG-TERM COSTS

GET RE-ELECTED

TO BE A POLITICIAN, YOU NEED TO LEARN HOW TO PROVE YOUR LOYALTY TO THE PEOPLE WHO FUND YOUR CAMPAIGNS AND THE PEOPLE WHO VOTE FOR YOU.

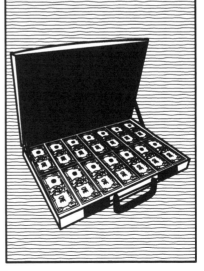

IN OTHER WORDS, YOU NEED TO BUILD A REPUTATION OF BEING A SELLOUT. THAT IS THE NATURE OF POLITICS. YOU NEED TO SELL OUT TO A PARTY, TO WEALTHY CAMPAIGN CONTRIBUTORS EXPECTING POLITICAL PAYBACK, AND YOU NEED TO SELL OUT TO THE PEOPLE WHO ARE GOING TO VOTE FOR YOU.

JUST TELL ME WHAT YOU WANT TO HEAR TO GET YOUR VOTE AND THAT'S WHAT I'LL SAY.

BUYING VOTES FROM THE SLAVES IS FOR THE MOST PART A GAME OF KEEP AWAY WITH THE SLAVES' OWN MONEY STOLEN TROUGH TAXES.

I'VE GOT SOMETHING OF YOURS.

TO ONE GROUP THEY SAY, I'LL TAX YOU LESS, AND TO ANOTHER GROUP THEY SAY, I'LL SPEND TAX DOLLARS ON YOU.

AND PEOPLE ACTUALLY FALL FOR THIS UTTER TRAVESTY. IT IS REALLY PATHETIC. IT IS PEOPLE CHEERING FOR BULLIES TOSSING AROUND THEIR OWN STOLEN MONEY IN A GAME OF KEEP AWAY.

I'LL GIVE IT BACK TO YOU...

NO, I'LL GIVE IT BACK TO YOU...

I ONLY WANT TO STEAL 20%.

DO PEOPLE HAVE NO DIGNITY?

DOING THE RIGHT THING IS NOT HOW TO BE A SUCCESSFUL POLITICIAN; YOU NEED TO BE A DISINGENUOUS CROOK. OTHER THAN THE OCCASIONAL FLUKE, THERE IS REALLY NO SUCH THING AS AN HONEST POLITICIAN.

AN HONEST PERSON IS SELF-CONSISTENT ENOUGH TO STEER CLEAR OF TELLING PEOPLE WHAT TO DO AT THE BARREL OF A GUN.

IF YOU BRING UP THE SUBJECT OF NO GOVERNMENT TO THE AVERAGE SLAVE, HE OR SHE WILL IMMEDIATELY GO INTO DEFEND GOVERNMENT MODE. AND SINCE THE SLAVES ARE SO UNIFORMLY BRAINWASHED, THE ARGUMENTS THEY COME UP WITH ARE QUITE PREDICTABLE.

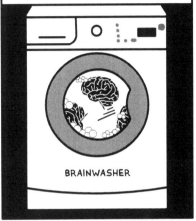

BRAINWASHER

THE WORST THING PEOPLE CAN OFTEN IMAGINE HAPPENING IN A SOCIETY FREE OF GOVERNMENT IS THAT SOME SORT OF ORGANIZED CRIME SYNDICATE WOULD TAKE OVER TO CONTROL EVERYONE.

IT WOULD FORM PROTECTION RACKETS AND FORCE PEOPLE TO PAY FOR PROTECTION. IT WOULD EXTORT PEOPLE AND MAKE THEM PAY UP TO GET AND KEEP A JOB. IT WOULD ALSO EXTORT PEOPLE AND MAKE THEM PAY UP TO STAY ON THEIR OWN PROPERTY. IT WOULD FORCE PEOPLE TO DO WORK THAT ONLY THE SYNDICATE APPROVED OF, SINCE IT WOULDN'T WANT COMPETITION. AND THE LIST OF HORRORS PEOPLE IMAGINE GOES ON AND ON.

THAT INDEED WOULD BE QUITE UNPLEASANT. THE ONLY PROBLEM IS, WHAT PEOPLE DESCRIBE IN SUCH A SCENARIO IS ACTUALLY EXACTLY WHAT A GOVERNMENT IS. THE ONLY DIFFERENCE IS THAT IN MANY GOVERNMENT SYSTEMS THE PEOPLE GET TO VOTE IN ELECTIONS BETWEEN SYNDICATE A AND SYNDICATE B.

AND SINCE PEOPLE DELUSIONALLY BELIEVE THAT THE CHOICE BETWEEN SYNDICATES MEANS THEY CONTROL THE SYNDICATES, THEY UNWITTINGLY THINK THAT WHAT THEY DO TO SUPPORT THE SYNDICATES IS IN THEIR OWN BEST INTEREST. THEREFORE, THEY ARE WILLING TO TATTLE ON PEOPLE AND SHEEPISHLY BOW DOWN TO THE DEMANDS OF THE SYNDICATES.

DEMOCRACY IS LIKE COWS VOTING ON HOW HIGH THE FENCES SHOULD BE. THERE ISN'T EVER A NO FENCES OPTION.

GOVERNMENT DOESN'T REALLY WORK. WHEN YOU GIVE AN ENTITY A MONOPOLY ON THE INITIATION OF FORCE, PEOPLE ARE GOING TO MISUSE THAT FORCE. AND NO MATTER HOW JUST YOU DELUSIONALLY THINK A PARTICULAR EXPRESSION OF THAT FORCE IS, THE PERSON ON THE OTHER SIDE OF THE FORCE IS GOING TO DISAGREE.

HOW DARE YOU CHALLENGE MY RIGHT TO BUDDY UP WITH THE GOVERNMENT AND USE ITS FORCE TO STEAL WEALTH!

GOVERNMENT IS JUST A CONSTANT FLUCTUATION BETWEEN DIFFERENT VARIATIONS OF "DOESN'T REALLY WORK." IT'S ALWAYS A GAME OF SLAVES AND MASTERS.

MASTERS

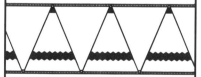

SLAVES

AND WHILE I, OF COURSE, USE THE TERMS OF SLAVES AND MASTERS FOR DRAMATIC EFFECT, IT IS NONETHELESS A TRUE ENOUGH DESCRIPTION OF GOVERNMENT SYSTEMS.

CHAPTER TWO

RAISING SLAVES

GOVERNMENT CLEARLY REPRESENTS A KIND OF SOCIETAL PARENT FIGURE. AND IN THE UNITED STATES, THAT PARENT FIGURE IS QUITE CLEARLY SPLIT INTO A MOTHER, REPRESENTED BY THE DEMOCRATIC PARTY, AND A FATHER, REPRESENTED BY THE REPUBLICAN PARTY.

MOTHER

FATHER

THE MOTHER TRIES TO CODDLE THE CHILDREN AND RESTRICT THEIR FREEDOM WITHIN THE HOME (HOMELAND), WHILE THE FATHER TRIES TO GO OUT AND CONQUER NEW LANDS AND BRING HOME THE PLUNDER OF THE HUNT.

IN OTHER WORDS, THE MOTHER IS THE SOCIALIST CORPORATIST WHILE THE FATHER IS THE MILITARIST CORPORATIST. BOTH HAVE CORPORATISM IN COMMON.

SOCIALIST CORPORATIST

MILITARIST CORPORATIST

THE DIFFERENCE ISN'T ALWAYS CLEAR, BUT THE MOTHER MOSTLY USES HER FORCE TO WAGE WARS AT HOME TO MAINTAIN DOMINANCE, WHILE THE FATHER HAS A PREFERENCE FOR WAGING WARS ABROAD.

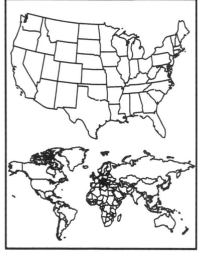

THIS MOTHER AND FATHER PARENT DYNAMIC FOUND IN GOVERNMENT IS NO ACCIDENT; IT IS A MANIFESTATION OF THE COLLECTIVE PSYCHOLOGY OF THE POPULATION.

THE GOVERNMENT IS THE IMAGINARY PARENT AND THE PEOPLE ARE ALL BROTHERS AND SISTERS: SIBLINGS.[1]

SINCE THE GOVERNMENT IS OUR SOCIETAL PARENT, CITIZENS AS CHILDREN LEARN HOW TO BEHAVE AND INTERACT AS THE PARENT BEHAVES AND INTERACTS.

39

SINCE GOVERNMENT BEHAVES AND INTERACTS USING THE INITIATION OF FORCE, CITIZENS LEARN TO BEHAVE AND INTERACT USING THE INITIATION OF FORCE.

MONKEY SEE MONKEY DO

HOWEVER, SINCE GOVERNMENT TRIES TO HOLD A MONOPOLY ON THE INITIATION OF FORCE, CITIZENS ARE REPRIMANDED FOR ACTING TOO MUCH LIKE THE GOVERNMENT. THE GOVERNMENT TRIES TO RAISE ITS CHILDREN BY TELLING THEM TO:

AN IMPLICIT **MIGHT MAKES RIGHT** DYNAMIC IS TAUGHT TO THE CHILDREN. THERE IS NO REASON OR EVIDENCE INVOLVED IN BEING RIGHT, JUST FORCE.

THE RESULT IS BASICALLY A CITIZENRY OF ABUSED CHILDREN THAT LEARN THAT MIGHT MAKES RIGHT, NOT REASON AND EVIDENCE.

40

AND SINCE THE ABUSED CHILDREN CAN'T RETALIATE AGAINST THE GOVERNMENT WITHOUT BACKLASH, THE CHILDREN INSTEAD INGRATIATE THEMSELVES WITH THE GOVERNMENT--USING AN APPEAL TO GOVERNMENT TO KEEP THEIR FELLOW ABUSED SIBLINGS IN LINE.

911 WHAT'S YOUR EMERGENCY? ARE SOME OF YOUR FELLOW SLAVES ACTING UP?

IN OTHER WORDS, IT BECOMES A GAME OF PSYCHOLOGICAL PROJECTION WHEREBY THE CHILDREN PROJECT THEIR OWN LEARNED THIRST FOR THE INITIATION OF FORCE ONTO THEIR SIBLINGS.

FORCE WAITING TO HAPPEN

THEREFORE, BASICALLY, THE GOVERNMENT RAISES ABUSED CHILDREN SO THAT THE CHILDREN WILL LOOK TO GOVERNMENT TO PROTECT THEM FROM THEMSELVES.

THE GOVERNMENT NEEDS TO STOP LETTING ME BE SUCH A PIG.

IT'S QUITE INSANE. BUT WHEN YOU REALLY LOOK AT IT, THAT IS INDEED THE GENERAL PSYCHOLOGICAL DYNAMIC REFLECTED BY A GOVERNMENT-RUN SOCIETY.

41

AND THAT SAME DYNAMIC IS NATURALLY ALSO REFLECTED IN MOST MAJOR RELIGIONS, WHEREBY GOD REPRESENTS THE ULTIMATE PARENT. GOD HAS A MONOPOLY ON FORCE AND THE CHILDREN OF GOD INGRATIATE THEMSELVES WITH GOD. THIS ALLOWS THE CHILDREN TO PROJECT THEIR OWN LEARNED THIRST FOR THE INITIATION OF FORCE ONTO OTHERS. THAT PROJECTION KEEPS THE FORCE SEEMINGLY IN OTHERS INSTEAD OF THE SELF, THUS SUSTAINING A TYRANNICAL, PUNISHING CONCEPT OF GOD.

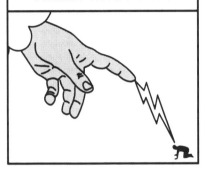

SO, WHETHER IT IS GOD OR GOVERNMENT, WHAT IT REALLY REPRESENTS IS A GHOST USED TO PROTECT OURSELVES FROM OURSELVES. BUT THE REASON WE FEAR OURSELVES TO BEGIN WITH IS BECAUSE WE SEE OURSELVES AS POSSESSING THE SAME QUALITIES AS THE TYRANNICAL GHOST WE MADE UP TO PROTECT OURSELVES.

MIRROR MIRROR ON THE WALL, WHO'S THE MOST STATELY SLAVE OF ALL?

IT IS AN INCREDIBLY INSANE LOOP. SO, IF YOU THINK WE NEED GOVERNMENT, IT IS A TELLTALE PSYCHOLOGICAL SIGN THAT BY BEING RAISED UNDER THE TYRANNY OF FORCE, YOU DEVELOPED AN INNER TYRANT YOU NOW PROJECT UPON YOUR FELLOW SLAVES.

THE EVIL YOU FEAR IN OTHERS IS MERELY THE EVIL YOU FEAR IN YOURSELF. NOW OBVIOUSLY, THIS BRINGS UP THE QUESTION OF WHAT CAME FIRST, THE TYRANNICAL GHOST OR THE REPRESSED INNER TYRANT?

LET ME OUT!

WELL, THE ANSWER IS THAT THEY ARE AN INTERDEPENDENT BINARY, LIKE TWO SIDES OF THE SAME COIN. SUCH A BINARY IS EXACTLY WHAT YOU'D EXPECT TO ARISE WHEN TRYING TO BALANCE THE IDEA THAT THE INITIATION OF FORCE IS WRONG WITH THE IDEA THAT THE INITIATION OF FORCE IS JUST.

IF THE INITIATION OF FORCE IS WRONG, IT IS NOT JUST. SO, WHETHER YOU TRY TO MAKE UP A GOVERNMENT, AN OMNIPOTENT DEITY, OR WHATEVER, AS LONG AS IT INITIATES FORCE BUT SAYS FORCE IS WRONG, YOU END UP WITH AN INSANE LOOP OF TYRANNICAL GHOST AND REPRESSED INNER TYRANT.

TYRANNICAL GHOST

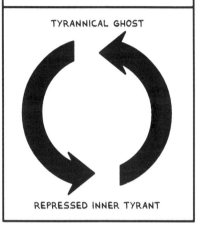

REPRESSED INNER TYRANT

THIS INSANE LOOP, RESULTING FROM TRYING TO HOLD TWO CONTRADICTING IDEAS AS TRUE, REPRESENTS A KIND OF METAPHORICAL MENTAL HELL. THEREFORE, THE ONE IDEA THAT IS TRUE REPRESENTS A METAPHORICAL MENTAL HEAVEN.

TYRANTS ARE REAL. BUT THE TYRANT IS IN OTHERS, NOT MYSELF. I NEED A TYRANT TO PROTECT ME.

THE IDEA THAT THE INITIATION OF FORCE IS WRONG IS THE TRUE IDEA AND THUS THE HEAVENLY IDEA.

THE ONLY TYRANT IS MY BELIEF IN TYRANTS. NO BELIEF IN INITIATING FORCE, I'M NOT A TYRANT.

43

WE KNOW IT IS TRUE BECAUSE IF INSTEAD THE INITIATION OF FORCE IS JUST, IT LEADS TO SELF-CONTRADICTIONS. OBVIOUSLY, BY DECLARING THE INITIATION OF FORCE AS JUST, YOU'VE SET UP THE CONDITIONS FOR YOUR OWN DESTRUCTION BY SAYING IT IS JUST FOR OTHERS TO INITIATE FORCE ON YOU. SUCH IS THE **PARANOIA** OF THE SLAVE.

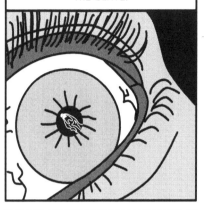

THE DEPTH OF THIS IDEA OF TRUTH BEING THAT WHICH CANNOT BE REDUCED INTO BINARIES OF SELF-CONTRADICTION IS SOMETHING THAT PERHAPS GETS DOWN TO THE VERY NATURE OF REALITY. BUT WE'LL EXPLORE THAT SUBJECT FURTHER WHEN WE GET TO THE CHAPTER ON WHAT IS TRUTH.

RIGHT
UP
BLACK
FULL

LEFT
DOWN
WHITE
EMPTY

OUR ACTUAL BIOLOGICAL PARENTS NOT ONLY HAD THEIR OWN BIOLOGICAL PARENTS, BUT WERE ALSO RAISED WITH THE GHOST PARENTS OF GODS AND GOVERNMENTS.

THEREFORE, IT IS NO SURPRISE THAT MOST PARENTS THEMSELVES END UP RAISING THEIR CHILDREN IN A WAY TAINTED BY THE INSANE, SELF-CONTRADICTING LOOP OF INITIATION OF FORCE IS WRONG AND INITIATION OF FORCE IS JUST.

INITIATION
OF FORCE
IS WRONG

INITIATION
OF FORCE
IS JUST

THIS IS MOST NOTABLY REFLECTED IN THE ARCHAIC PRACTICE OF CORPORAL PUNISHMENT. WHEN THE INITIATION OF FORCE IS USED TO TEACH WHAT IS RIGHT AND WRONG, ALL THAT IS REALLY TAUGHT IS THAT **MIGHT MAKES RIGHT**.

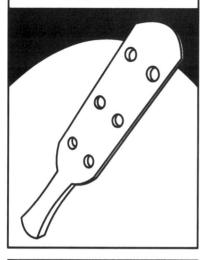

IF YOU REALLY WANT TO TEACH RIGHT AND WRONG, YOU APPEAL TO REASON, LOGIC, EVIDENCE, AND MOST OF ALL EXAMPLE, NOT SELF-CONTRADICTION THROUGH THE INITIATION OF FORCE.

IN OTHER WORDS, YOU TEACH THE CHILD TO ACTUALLY THINK. AND WHEN YOU TEACH YOUR CHILD TO ACTUALLY THINK, YOUR CHILD IS SMART ENOUGH TO NOT NEED DISCIPLINED.

AND IF YOU STILL THINK YOU NEED TO DISCIPLINE A CHILD THAT KNOWS HOW TO THINK, THEN YOU ARE THE DUMB ONE THAT NEEDS PUT IN LINE.

A COMMON REFRAIN FROM PEOPLE WHO USE CORPOREAL PUNISHMENT ON THEIR CHILDREN IS:

I WAS BEAT AS A KID AND I TURNED OUT FINE.

BUT THE TRUTH IS, PEOPLE WHO ACTUALLY TURNED OUT FINE DON'T BEAT THEIR CHILDREN. YOU NEED TO BE THE PARENT THAT YOU'D WANT TO HAVE YOURSELF.

AND THE SAME APPLIES TO THINGS LIKE GOD AND THE GOVERNMENT. YOU NEED TO BE THE GOD THAT YOU'D WANT TO HAVE YOURSELF. YOU NEED TO BE THE GOVERNMENT THAT YOU'D WANT TO HAVE YOURSELF.

UNLESS YOU ARE SOME KIND OF SICKO, YOU PROBABLY DON'T WANT A PARENT THAT IS GOING TO ABUSE YOU AND LOCK YOU UP. YOU PROBABLY DON'T WANT A GOD THAT'S GOING TO SEND YOU TO HELL AND SCREW WITH YOU TO PROVE YOUR LOYALTY. AND YOU PROBABLY DON'T WANT A GOVERNMENT THAT'S GOING TO MAKE YOU A SLAVE OR OUTRIGHT IMPRISON YOU.

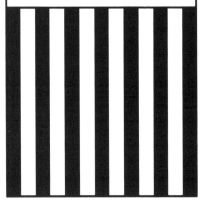

THE PARENT, GOD, AND GOVERNMENT YOU WANT IS ONE THAT KNOWS AND STANDS BY THE TRUTH WITH SUCH COMMITMENT THAT YOUR OWN ERRORS AND LIES ARE NEVER VALIDATED THROUGH A CONTRADICTION LIKE FORCEFUL PUNISHMENT; YOUR ERRORS AND LIES ARE ONLY CORRECTED, NOTHING MORE, NOTHING LESS.

GOVERNMENT WAS A CRAZY THING TO DO. YET, IT WAS NOTHING BUT A GHOST. IT WAS ALL JUST IN YOUR MIND.

IN OTHER WORDS, THE ONLY WORTHY AUTHORITY IS THE UNREALIZED TRUTH. WHEN TRUTH IS REALIZED THOUGH, IT IS NO LONGER AN AUTHORITY BUT AN EQUAL.

THE UNREALIZED TRUTH

YOU ARE WORTHY.

YOU ARE A WORTHY AUTHORITY.

EDUCATION SHOULD IDEALLY BE ABOUT THE PURSUIT OF TRUTH. BUT MUCH OF WHAT PASSES FOR EDUCATION IN THIS WORLD IS MORE AKIN TO INDOCTRINATION THAN EDUCATION.

I PLEDGE ALLEGIANCE TO A PIECE OF CLOTH THAT ACTS AS THE LOGO OF MY TAX FARM...

AND WHAT ELSE WOULD YOU EXPECT FROM A GOVERNMENT-HAUNTED WORLD? IT NEEDS TO KEEP EVERYONE BELIEVING IN ITS GHOSTS AFTER ALL.

BY ABOUT THE AGE OF FIVE, MOST CHILDREN BEGIN SOMETHING CALLED FORMAL EDUCATION. AND FORMAL EDUCATION IS OF COURSE MADE FORMAL BY BEING GOVERNMENT APPROVED.

MOST EDUCATION PEOPLE RECEIVE WHILE GROWING UP IS NOT REALLY ABOUT DEVELOPING INTELLIGENCE BUT INSTEAD HAS MORE TO DO WITH DEVELOPING OBEDIENCE AND CONTROL; IT'S ABOUT CULTURALIZATION.

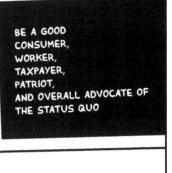

BE A GOOD CONSUMER, WORKER, TAXPAYER, PATRIOT, AND OVERALL ADVOCATE OF THE STATUS QUO

I DON'T DEFINE INTELLIGENCE AS BEING ABLE TO OBEDIENTLY REGURGITATE INFORMATION LIKE A COMPUTER, OR BEING ABLE TO FIT INTO A SICK SOCIETY. INTELLIGENCE IS CREATIVE, KIND, EMPATHETIC, AND BY NECESSITY SUBVERSIVE.

INTELLIGENCE IS REALLY ANTITHETICAL TO THE STANDARD PUBLIC EDUCATION SYSTEM. AFTER ALL, THE WHOLE PUBLIC EDUCATION SYSTEM IS FOUNDED ON THE INITIATION OF FORCE.

48

THAT FORCE STARTS WITH THE FACT THAT PUBLIC EDUCATION GETS ITS FUNDING THROUGH TAXATION, WHICH IS COLLECTED USING THE THREAT OF FORCE. TAXATION IS THE CHARITY EQUIVALENT OF RAPE. YOU GET WHAT TAXATION PAYS FOR WHETHER YOU WANT IT OR NOT. SO, EDUCATION FUNDING IS NOT VOLUNTARY. NOT CONSCIOUSLY VOLUNTARY THAT IS--SINCE MOST PEOPLE HAVE BEEN UNCONSCIOUSLY BRAINWASHED TO ACCEPT IT WITHOUT QUESTION.

BUT WITHOUT GOVERNMENT WHO WOULD EDUCATE KIDS?

AND NOT ONLY IS THE FUNDING NOT VOLUNTARY, CHILD PARTICIPATION IN THE SYSTEM IS NOT REALLY VOLUNTARY EITHER.

GET ON THE BUS!

EVEN PRIVATE SCHOOLS, WHICH TEND TO BE EXPENSIVE SINCE THEY HAVE TO COMPETE WITH THE PUBLIC EDUCATION MONOPOLY, HAVE TO CONFORM TO GOVERNMENT REGULATIONS. WHICH MEANS THEY CAN'T BE TOO DIFFERENT FROM PUBLIC EDUCATION.

SO, MOST PEOPLE GET EDUCATED IN AN INVOLUNTARY PRISON-LIKE SYSTEM WHERE A STATE-SANCTIONED AUTHORITATIVE FIGURE KNOWN AS A TEACHER ATTEMPTS TO INSTILL OBEDIENCE BY IMPLICITLY SAYING:

DON'T THINK FOR YOURSELF, THINK WHAT I SAY IS RIGHT.

49

ALL THE WHILE, THERE'S A LORD OF THE FLIES QUALITY TO THE FACT THAT ALL THESE KIDS ARE CORRALLED INTO THE SAME PLOT OF LAND EVERY DAY. THEREFORE, THE SCHOOLYARD SOCIAL SYSTEM TENDS TO ALWAYS DEVOLVE INTO COMPLIANCE WITH THE LOWEST COMMON DENOMINATOR.

GROUP OF SCHOOL CHILDREN

LOWEST COMMON DENOMINATORS = BULLIES, PHYSICALLY ATTRACTIVE, ATHLETIC

AND THAT IS WHAT PASSES FOR EDUCATION IN CONTEMPORARY SOCIETY. IT IS ACTUALLY QUITE ARCHAIC, SEEING AS A SUPERIOR, VOLUNTARY, SELF-DIRECTED EDUCATION EXISTS VIRTUALLY FREE ON THE INTERNET THESE DAYS.

HOW TO KILL TIME AT SCHOOL:

BATHROOM BREAK EXAMPLE: 180 SCHOOL DAYS, MULTIPLIED BY 7 HOURS A DAY, MULTIPLIED BY 5 MINUTES PER HOUR ON BATHROOM BREAK=6,300 MINUTES OR (6300/60) 105 HOURS OR (105/7) 15 DAYS LESS OF SCHOOL A YEAR.

OTHER EXAMPLES:
* 10 MINUTES OF ORGANIZING PER DAY.
* 20 MINUTES OF SHARPENING PENCILS PER DAY (SMILE WHILE SHARPENING).
* 10 MINUTES OF STARING AT PEOPLE UNTIL THEY LOOK OVER AT YOU PER DAY.
* 10 MINUTES PER DAY TRYING TO MAKE THE PERFECT PAPER AIRPLANE.
* 15 MINUTES PER DAY UNDERLINING FUNNY, DOUBLE ENTENDRE WORDS IN BOOKS AND MAGAZINES.
* 20 MINUTES PER DAY TURNING TEXTBOOK PICTURES INTO HUMOROUS COMICS.

IF ALL THE MONEY SPENT ON EDUCATING KIDS EACH YEAR WAS SPENT ON VOLUNTARY FREE MARKET EDUCATION, MOST KIDS WOULD END UP LOVING LEARNING. IT WOULD LIKELY SIMPLY INVOLVE THINGS LIKE PLAYING FUN, EXCITING, EDUCATIONAL VIDEO GAMES AT ONE'S OWN PACE WITHOUT HAVING TO LEAVE THE COMFORT OF HOME.

YOU HAVE NOW COMPLETED THIRD GRADE. CONGRATULATIONS!

LRB   PONY

IT WOULD ALSO LIKELY INCLUDE ACTUALLY BUILDING AND PRODUCING THINGS.

INSTEAD, KIDS ARE SENT TO WHAT AMOUNTS TO A STATE-RUN DAYCARE PRISON PROGRAM THAT ALLOWS THE PARENTS TO GO TO WORK WHILE THE KIDS GET BRAINWASHED...I MEAN EDUCATED.

REFERENCE TO PINK FLOYD'S THE WALL

50

OF COURSE, SEEING AS MOST PARENTS WERE THEMSELVES EDUCATED IN THE STANDARD STATE SYSTEM, THEY THEMSELVES NEVER BECAME SMART ENOUGH TO SEE THROUGH THE SYSTEM. THEY SEE IT AS NORMAL AND JUST COMPLY WITH IT.

BUT THE FACT THAT MOST KIDS EVENTUALLY DETEST HAVING TO GO TO SCHOOL GOES TO SHOW THAT THERE IS SOMETHING WRONG WITH THE SYSTEM.

AND TO ADD INSULT TO INJURY, SCHOOLS GIVE HOMEWORK. AS IF SPENDING EVERY DAY DEALING WITH THE EXCRUCIATING ROTE DRIVEL ISN'T BAD ENOUGH, KIDS HAVE TO BRING IT HOME TO IMPEDE ON THE LITTLE TIME THEY HAVE FOR THINGS LIKE FAMILY AND INDULGING IN INTERESTS THAT AREN'T DIRECTLY SCHOOL RELATED.

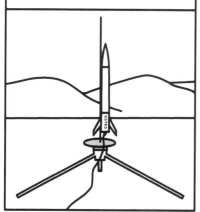

EVEN IF A KID IS ABLE TO COPE WITH THE OBEDIENCE PART, THE LORD OF THE FLIES PART IS OFTEN TOO MUCH.

AND EVEN IF A KID IS ABLE TO COPE WITH THE LORD OF THE FLIES PART, THE OBEDIENCE PART IS OFTEN TOO MUCH.

HOW CAN YOU HAVE ANY PUDDING IF YOU DON'T EAT YOUR MEAT?

SO, WHAT THE EDUCATION SYSTEM ENDS UP INCUBATING IS MOSTLY BULLIES AND SUCK-UPS.

GIVE ME ALL YOUR FREE TIME TONIGHT BY DOING THIS POINTLESS HOMEWORK!

YES TEACHER. IS THAT ALL?

WHAT WE REALLY LEARN FROM OUR TEACHERS IS NOT WHAT THEY TEACH US INTELLECTUALLY. WHAT WE REALLY LEARN FROM OUR TEACHERS IS HOW THEY TREAT US. THEREFORE, WHAT WE REMEMBER ABOUT OUR TEACHERS IS WHETHER THEY WERE MEAN, NICE, OR NEUTRAL.

TAKE A MOMENT TO THINK BACK TO ALL THE TEACHERS YOU HAD. I DOUBT YOU CAN THINK OF MUCH EACH TEACHER SPECIFICALLY TAUGHT YOU, BUT YOU PROBABLY DO REMEMBER IF THE TEACHER WAS NICE OR MEAN.

AND IN GENERAL, SINCE THE WHOLE STRUCTURE OF EDUCATION **REVOLVES** AROUND BULLYING THE KIDS TO DO WHAT THEY ARE TOLD WHEN THEY ARE TOLD, KIDS LEARN EITHER TO BE BULLIES, LIKE THE SYSTEM ITSELF, OR SUCK-UPS COMPLIANT WITH THE SYSTEM.

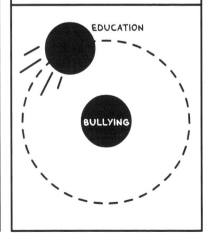

EDUCATION

BULLYING

THE BULLIES BECOME THE BOSSES AND LAW ENFORCERS, AS WELL AS THE CRIMINALS; YOU NEED BOTH TO HAVE THE OTHER. AND THE SUCK-UPS BECOME THE BUREAUCRATS. THEY ALL EXIST TO TOUT THE STATUS QUO.

THEN THERE ARE THE FEW PEOPLE WHO MANAGE TO ADAPT TO BOTH THE LORD OF THE FLIES ASPECT OF SCHOOL AS WELL AS THE OBEDIENCE ASPECT TO BECOME GOOD-LOOKING, ASS-KISSING BULLIES THAT GET STRAIGHT A'S: THE IDEAL POLITICIAN OR SALESPERSON.

SAVOR MY B.S.

I'M OBVIOUSLY BEING PURPOSELY FACETIOUS AND SIMPLISTIC IN THIS ACCOUNT, BUT IT'S NONETHELESS PRECISELY WHAT ONE WOULD EXPECT FROM A COERCIVE, AUTHORITATIVE, STATE-RUN SYSTEM.

WHAT A REAL EDUCATION SYSTEM WOULD INCUBATE IS BASICALLY A BUNCH OF SOCRATIC GADFLIES: PEOPLE WHO QUESTION THE STATUS QUO BY THINKING CRITICALLY FOR THEMSELVES.

POURQUOI

BUT WHY?

THAT MAKES NO SENSE.

BUT A STATE-RUN SYSTEM, WHETHER INTENTIONALLY OR INSTINCTIVELY, DOESN'T WANT PEOPLE TO BECOME SMART ENOUGH TO SEE THROUGH THE SYSTEM.

SO, OVERALL, DESPITE ANY DELUSIONS OF GOOD INTENTIONS BY WELL-MEANING EDUCATORS, THE POWER STRUCTURE OF STANDARD EDUCATION SIMPLY REINFORCES THE SELF-CONTRADICTION OF FORCE IS WRONG BUT FORCE IS JUST.

AND DESPITE THE UTTER LACK OF LOGIC IT ENTAILS, THAT'S WHAT IS NEEDED TO RAISE SLAVES. IF WE CAN'T TEACH CHILDREN THE LOGIC OF NON-AGGRESSION WITHOUT CONTRADICTING OURSELVES, WE CAN'T TEACH THE MORALITY AND ETHICS NEEDED FOR PEACE...AND IN TURN A VOLUNTARYIST SOCIETY.

I'M OF COURSE WILLING TO CONCEDE THAT MANY PARENTS ARE MUCH WORSE THAN THE STATE SCHOOL SYSTEM. THUS, SOME CHILDREN COME FROM HOMES SO BAD, AND IMPOVERISHED, AND ABUSIVE THAT PUBLIC SCHOOL IS COMPARATIVELY AN OASIS.

HOWEVER, IT COULD BE ARGUED THAT SUCH A CHILD WOULD BE BETTER OFF IF HE OR SHE HAD THE FREEDOM TO RUN AWAY, GET A JOB, AND LIVE WITH NEW PEOPLE OF HIS OR HER OWN CHOOSING. THAT'S A RELATIVELY WEIRD IDEA, BUT SO IS PICKING A SET AGE TO CONSIDER A KID AN ADULT.

SCHOOL IS SLAVE LABOR COMPARED TO SOMETHING LIKE WORKING IN A FACTORY. GOVERNMENT FORCES KIDS TO GO TO SCHOOL. AND WHILE GOVERNMENT PAYS THE TEACHERS, ADMINISTRATORS, BUILDERS OF THE SCHOOLS, BUS DRIVERS, AND EVERYONE ELSE, IT DOESN'T PAY THE KIDS.

THE MANDATED EDUCATION IS CONSIDERED THE PAYMENT...AND I GUESS SOME KIDS GET STUFF LIKE FREE LUNCHES AND FREE BUS RIDES IF YOU WANT TO CONSIDER THAT PAYMENT.

PUBLIC SCHOOL IS HOW YOU RAISE SLAVES, NOT FREE PEOPLE. I'M PERSONALLY NOT A PRODUCT OF PUBLIC SCHOOL. I WENT TO PUBLIC SCHOOL BRIEFLY TWICE, BUT WENT TO PRIVATE SCHOOL THE REST OF THE TIME. AT PRIVATE SCHOOL WE ACTUALLY LEARNED ABOUT THINGS LIKE MORALITY, ETHICS, AND PHILOSOPHY.

55

HOWEVER, SINCE PRIVATE SCHOOLS ARE ALSO GOVERNMENT REGULATED, THEY ARE ONLY SLIGHTLY MORE FREE AND CONDUCIVE TO RAISING FREE-MINDED PEOPLE.

EVEN COLLEGE GRADUATES USUALLY NEVER LEARN TO SEE THROUGH THE DECEPTIONS OF THE GOVERNMENT SYSTEM. PART OF THAT HAS TO DO WITH THE FACT THAT MANY COLLEGES ARE FUNDED BY THE GOVERNMENT.

PRIVATE COLLEGES USUALLY ALSO FAIL TO PROPERLY EDUCATE. MANY PRIVATE COLLEGES ARE CORPORATIST FUNDED INSTITUTIONS, WHICH IS BASICALLY THE SAME AS BEING GOVERNMENT FUNDED.

IF YOU ARE READING THIS BOOK AS PART OF A COLLEGE COURSE, THEN YOUR PROFESSOR IS QUITE COOL.

56

THE ONLY REASON I WENT TO COLLEGE BEYOND MY FRESHMAN YEAR IS BECAUSE I HAD A SCHOLARSHIP. I'VE NEVER HAD INTEREST IN EMPLOYMENT, ONLY FREE MARKETS AND LIVING LIFE FREELY. SO, I'VE NEVER WORRIED ABOUT PROVING ANYTHING TO ANYONE WITH A MAGIC PIECE OF PAPER.

IF I WANTED TO PLAY THE PROFESSIONAL GAME AND BECOME A DOCTOR OR PROFESSOR, I WOULD HAVE HAD TO BE MORE DEDICATED TO COLLEGE EDUCATION.

BUT OVERALL, I CAN SAY WITH CONFIDENCE THAT IF A PERSON JUST STARTED READING ONE NONFICTION BOOK A WEEK AT AGE 18, IN FOUR YEARS, THAT PERSON WOULD LIKELY BE IVY LEAGUE SMART. AND IF YOU ARE 18 AND HAVE NO INTEREST IN READING BOOKS, THEN THERE IS NO POINT IN GOING TO COLLEGE ANYWAY.

WHAT YOU HAVE TO KEEP IN MIND ABOUT COLLEGE IS THAT A PLACE LIKE HARVARD DOESN'T REALLY MAKE PEOPLE SMART. HARVARD MOSTLY ONLY ACCEPTS PEOPLE WHO ARE SMART TO BEGIN WITH.

FROST, HEARST, GATES, BUCKMINSTER FULLER, ZUCKERBERG ALL DROPPED OUT OF HARVARD, BUT TED KACZYNSKI GRADUATED.

IT IS UNDERSTANDABLE THAT A PROFESSOR, OR A COLLEGE ADMINISTRATOR, WOULD WANT TO DEFEND THE UTTER IMPORTANCE OF A COLLEGE DEGREE. BUT THAT'S JUST BECAUSE SUCH PEOPLE ARE INVESTED IN THAT WORLDVIEW AND DON'T WANT TO LOSE THEIR JOBS OR PUT THE VALUE OF WHAT THEY TEACH UP TO FREE MARKET FORCES.

AFTER ALL, YOU DON'T HEAR TOO MANY PROFESSORS COMPLAINING ABOUT TENURE. THE INTENDED PURPOSE OF TENURE WAS ORIGINALLY TO PROTECT EDUCATORS WITH CONTROVERSIAL IDEAS.

HOWEVER, WHAT TENURE REALLY DOES IS KEEP CONTROVERSIAL PEOPLE FROM EVER GETTING EDUCATION JOBS TO BEGIN WITH. IF HIRING SOMEONE MEANS THE POTENTIAL OF BEING STUCK WITH THAT PERSON INDEFINITELY, IT'S SAFEST TO GO WITH THE STATUS QUO PERSON.

I THINK MY COLLEAGUES ARE FULL OF IT AND ARE JUST FOLLOWING THE HERD TO FURTHER THEIR CAREERS.

TENURE THUS RUINS THE FEEDBACK MECHANISM THAT WOULD REWARD TRULY RADICAL THINKERS BY BRINGING IN MORE STUDENTS.

I WANT TO GO THE OPPOSITE DIRECTION WITH MY WORK TO SHOW THAT MY COLLEAGUES ARE ALL WRONG. WHY CAN'T I GET TENURE LIKE THEM?

58

BUT ENOUGH ABOUT COLLEGE. UNTIL COLLEGES WIDELY TEACH THE KINDS OF IDEAS IN THIS BOOK, IT IS SAFE TO SAY THEY ARE JUST A CONTINUATION OF THE SLAVE SYSTEM.

A SLAVE IS RAISED TO ACCEPT VIOLENCE--TO ACCEPT CONTRADICTION. A FREE PERSON IS RAISED FREE OF VIOLENCE, AND WITH A GREAT AWARENESS OF THE SELF-CONTRADICTION VIOLENCE ENTAILS.

I'M A LITTLE KID AND I KNOW NOT TO STEAL, HURT, OR LIE. WHY DOESN'T THE GOVERNMENT?

THE RISE OF VOLUNTARYISM DEPENDS ON PEOPLE RAISING NON-VIOLENT CHILDREN WHO ARE SMART ENOUGH AND EMPATHETIC ENOUGH TO SEE THROUGH THE VIOLENCE INHERENT IN GOVERNMENT.

MR. VOLUNTARY SAYS:

ALWAYS REMEMBER: GARBAGE IN MEANS GARBAGE OUT.

BUT INSTEAD, CHILDREN ARE TRAINED TO BE LOYAL PATRIOTS AND AGGRESSORS.

LOOK AT THE GOVERNMENT-FRIENDLY PROPAGANDA IN THE ADULATION OF SPORTS IN SOCIETY. JUST BECAUSE YOU LIVE IN SOME GEOGRAPHICAL AREA, YOU ARE SUPPOSED TO SUPPORT A CERTAIN SPORTS TEAM.

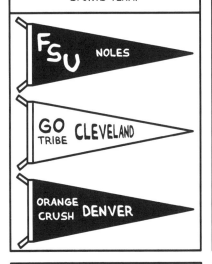

AND BY BEING ON A TEAM, REGARDLESS OF WHERE YOU ARE REALLY FROM, YOU REPRESENT A GEOGRAPHICAL AREA.

I'M A REF, AND LIKE THE GOVERNMENT, WHAT I SAY IS TRUTH...REGARDLESS OF WHAT YOU MIGHT THINK.

SPORTS ARE FUN, BUT ON A DEEPER LEVEL, IT'S ALL JUST SUBTLE CONDITIONING TO ENCOURAGE AND FEED WARMONGERING AND TRIBAL IDENTIFICATION.

WHICH BRINGS US TO OUR NEXT SUBJECT, WAR.

CHAPTER THREE

WAR

THE HEALTH AND GROWTH OF GOVERNMENT IS WAR.

GOVERNMENTS CAN OBVIOUSLY GROW BY FORCEFULLY TAKING OVER OTHER GOVERNMENTS THROUGH WAR. BUT GOVERNMENTS CAN ALSO GROW BY FORCEFULLY TAKING OVER THEIR OWN CITIZENRY THROUGH WAR. SUCH WARS ARE KNOWN AS THINGS LIKE WARS ON DRUGS, WARS ON POVERTY, WARS ON POLLUTION, WARS ON TERROR...

WARS ARE THE GOVERNMENT'S SOLUTION TO PROBLEMS THE GOVERNMENT CREATES.

DEFAULT GOVERNMENT SOLUTION

WARS IN THE TRADITIONAL SENSE OF GOVERNMENTS FIGHTING OTHER GOVERNMENTS ARE THE RESULT OF THE EXISTENCE OF GOVERNMENTS TO BEGIN WITH. FIRST OFF, IT TAKES A MONOPOLY ON FORCE TO EXTRACT THE RESOURCES FROM A GROUP OF PEOPLE TO BUILD AN AGGRESSING MILITARY OF ANY SIGNIFICANCE.

ECONOMICALLY, WAR MAKES NO SENSE EXCEPT TO GOVERNMENT AND CORPORATISTS. WITHOUT THE DISTORTIONS OF GOVERNMENT, WAR BEYOND SELF-DEFENSE IS WAY TOO RISKY, WAY TOO EXPENSIVE, COUNTERPRODUCTIVE, AND WAY TOO UNREASONABLE TO GET FUNDING AND PARTICIPATION THAT OUTWEIGHS RESISTANCE.

FURTHERMORE, IT'S VERY DIFFICULT TO GO INTO A POPULATION OF PEOPLE AND TAKE OVER UNLESS THERE IS AN EXISTING GOVERNMENT STRUCTURE TO TAKE OVER.

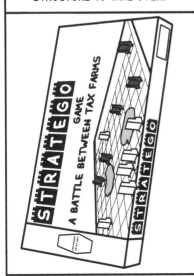

IN OTHER WORDS, WAR IS ONLY APPEALING AND REASONABLY FEASIBLE IF IT MEANS ONE GOVERNMENT TAKING OVER AN EXISTING GOVERNMENT: ONE TAX COLLECTION SCHEME TAKING OVER ANOTHER TAX COLLECTION SCHEME.

IN THE BIG PICTURE, WARS ONLY ARISE BECAUSE THERE ARE PEOPLE WILLING TO FIGHT IN THEM. WHICH IS TO SAY, THERE ARE SLAVES SO DEEPLY CONDITIONED BY GOVERNMENT PROPAGANDA THAT THEY ARE WILLING TO RISK LIFE AND LIMB FOR WHAT AMOUNTS TO FIGHTING FOR A CERTAIN BRAND OF SLAVERY.

BE READY!

JOIN NOW

THE FACT IS THAT SUPPORT OF THE MILITARY WITHOUT PARTICIPATION IS EXPLOITIVE COWARDICE AND PARTICIPATION IN THE MILITARY IS OBSEQUIOUS WARMONGERING. I'M JUST EARNING A PAYCHECK IS NO EXCUSE.

AND WHILE I KNOW STATING THAT FACT WON'T WIN ME MANY POINTS WITH THE MILITARY OR WITH THE MANY PANDERING PATRIOTS OF THE WORLD, SOMEONE HAS TO HAVE THE COJONES TO SAY IT, BECAUSE IT IS TRUE.

IF YOU, THE READER, ARE IN THE MILITARY OR HAVE SOME KIND OF AFFILIATION WITH IT THAT'S FINE. SOMETIMES THE MILITARY IS SIMPLY DEFENDING AGAINST AGGRESSORS. THERE'S NOTHING WRONG WITH THAT. BUT I'M STILL MAKING A PLEA FOR YOU TO RETHINK IT ALL.

EVEN WITH A SO-CALLED WORTHY CAUSE, LIKE FREEING SLAVES THROUGH THE U.S. CIVIL WAR, WAR IS UNNECESSARY. ALL SLAVERY DEPENDS ON A MONOPOLY ON INITIATING FORCE. IF IT WASN'T FOR GOVERNMENT USING STOLEN RESOURCES (TAXES) TO ENFORCE SLAVERY, THE SLAVES THEMSELVES WOULD HAVE TURNED ON THEIR MASTERS USING SELF-DEFENSE, AND THAT WOULD HAVE BEEN THE END OF THE SLAVERY.

63

PEACE IS NOT FOUND THROUGH WAR AND NEVER WILL BE. IT IS THE END OF THE INITIATION OF FORCE THAT ESTABLISHES PEACE. INSANE REACTIONS TO INSANITY DON'T ADD UP TO SANITY.

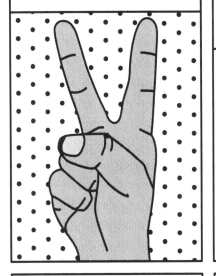

ANY WAR THAT RESULTS IN JUST MORE GOVERNMENT OF SOME FORM IS INEVITABLY A POINTLESS WAR. WHICH IS BASICALLY TO SAY THAT ALL WAR IS POINTLESS. WAR IS THE KIND OF NONSENSE THAT ONLY MAKES SENSE TO SLAVES THAT WERE NEVER TAUGHT HOW TO THINK, REASON, AND EMPATHIZE.

THE KITSCH ART of WAR

ZANDER MARZ

ONE THING YOU CAN REST ASSURED OF ABOUT A VOLUNTARYIST SOCIETY IS THAT IT WILL NEVER COME INTO EXISTENCE THROUGH VIOLENCE. THAT WOULD CONTRADICT THE WHOLE PREMISE.

A VOLUNTARYIST SOCIETY WILL ONLY COME INTO EXISTENCE THROUGH THE ABANDONMENT OF VIOLENCE: THE ABANDONMENT OF THE LOGICAL IMMORALITY OF THE INITIATION OF FORCE. A VOLUNTARYIST SOCIETY WILL COME INTO EXISTENCE WHEN THE SLAVES STOP OBEYING THE MASTERS.

GOVERNMENT SAYS:

CIVIL DISOBEDIENCE IS STILL DISOBEDIENCE

64

TO PRIVATIZE WAR IS SIMPLY TO MIMIC THE INITIATION OF FORCE PRACTICED BY GOVERNMENT.

IS JUST TERRORISM WITH A BIGGER BUDGET...THANKS TO FIAT MONEY AND DEBT.

WHETHER IT BE SOMETHING LIKE THE VIOLENCE OF THE 1992 L.A. RIOTS OR THE VIOLENCE OF THE 2001 911 ATTACKS, THE NET RESULT IS ONLY EVER JUST MORE GOVERNMENT AND THUS MORE VIOLENCE--HENCE THE **WAR ON TERROR**.

THE OTHER KIND OF WAR GOVERNMENTS USE TO STAY HEALTHY AND GROW IS INTERNALIZED WAR. SUCH WARS POSE TO USE GOVERNMENT TO SOLVE A PROBLEM WITHIN A COUNTRY. THE PROBLEM IN TURN IS THEN SUSTAINED BY THE SUPPOSED GOVERNMENT SOLUTION.

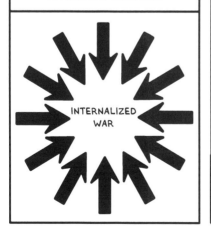

INTERNALIZED WAR

IN SUCH A WAR, VICTORY WOULD MEAN THE END OF THE WAR AND THUS THE END OF THE HEALTH AND GROWTH OF THE GOVERNMENT.

WE CAN DO IT...

...ENDLESSLY HARASS AND MANIPULATE CITIZENRY INTO GIVING UP MORE AND MORE POWER TO GOVERNMENT.

GOVERNMENT SOLUTIONS TO PROBLEMS LEAD TO FEEDBACK MECHANISMS THAT KEEP THE PROBLEM ALIVE.

CREATE OR IDENTIFY A PROBLEM

MAKE THE PROBLEM WORSE

GIVE GOVERNMENT POWER TO SOLVE PROBLEM

TAKE THE **WAR ON POVERTY** AS AN EXAMPLE. MOST GOVERNMENTS SPEND A LOT OF MONEY TRYING TO HELP THE IMPOVERISHED, YET POVERTY REMAINS.

TECHNOLOGY, WHICH IS MOSTLY A PRODUCT OF FREE ENTERPRISE, IS THE THING THAT HAS MADE POOR PEOPLE RICHER OVER TIME.

NEED MONEY TO PAY MY CELL PHONE BILL

ALL THE GOVERNMENT'S WAR ON POVERTY DOES IS CREATE FEEDBACK MECHANISMS TO SUSTAIN A DEPENDENT CLASS OF PEOPLE ASSURED TO STAY POOR ENOUGH TO REMAIN ON GOVERNMENT ASSISTANCE AND VOTE FOR THOSE WHO SUPPORT GOVERNMENT ASSISTANCE.

INSUFFICIENT PRODUCTIVE CAPITAL FOR ECONOMIC MOBILITY

NO GOOD INCENTIVE TO ACCUMULATE PRODUCTIVE CAPITAL

BASICS SUPPLIED THROUGH GOVERNMENT ASSISTANCE

THE WAR ON POVERTY USES THE VIOLENCE OF THE GOVERNMENT TO STEAL MONEY FROM PEOPLE WITH MONEY, THROUGH TAXATION, TO SUSTAIN A CLASS OF PEOPLE WILLING TO SUPPORT A NEVER-ENDING WAR ON POVERTY.

AND A LOT OF THAT MONEY ISN'T REALLY ABOUT HELPING THE POOR, IT IS ABOUT CORPORATE WELFARE.

BENEFIT SECURITY CARD

TAKE FOOD STAMPS AS A PRIME EXAMPLE. OBVIOUSLY, FOOD VENDORS AND PRODUCERS ARE NOT GOING TO COMPLAIN ABOUT FOOD STAMPS SINCE THEY ARE THE ONES WHO END UP WITH FOOD STAMP MONEY ONCE THE RECIPIENTS SPEND IT.

LIQUOR
CIGARETTES BEER
WE ACCEPT FOOD STAMPS EBT

WHAT IS REALLY UNFORTUNATE ABOUT THE WAR ON POVERTY SCAM IS THAT THERE ARE PLENTY OF PEOPLE WITH PLENTY OF MONEY THAT THINK THAT BY PAYING THEIR TAXES THEY ARE HELPING THE POOR. ALL THEY ARE DOING IS HELPING THE POOR STAY POOR AND THE POLITICALLY CONNECTED STAY WEALTHY.

67

PLUS, IT MESSES UP THE FAMILY DYNAMIC BY REPLACING FATHERS IN FAMILIES WITH GOVERNMENT. THUS, MANY POOR CHILDREN ARE RAISED BY SINGLE MOTHERS. AND THE STATS FOR CHILDREN RAISED WITHOUT FATHERS ARE QUITE BAD.

THE WAR ON POVERTY IS JUST A DISGUISE FOR ALL THE STUFF GOVERNMENT DOES TO MAKE POVERTY TO BEGIN WITH.

IN A COMPLETELY FREE SOCIETY AND THUS FREE ECONOMY, WHICH WE WILL EXPLORE IN MORE DETAIL LATER, THE ONLY WAY A PERSON COULD BE POOR IS IF THE PERSON DIDN'T WANT TO WORK AT ALL OR COULDN'T WORK AND DIDN'T HAVE ANY FAMILY OR FRIENDS WILLING TO SHARE THE WEALTH.

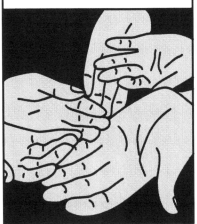

IN OTHER WORDS, POVERTY WOULD EITHER BE A CHOICE OR SO RARE THAT THERE WOULD BE MORE THAN ENOUGH CHARITY TO HELP TRUE CHARITY CASES.

GIVE

AN OFFSHOOT OF THE WAR ON POVERTY COULD BE DESCRIBED AS THE **WAR ON FREE MARKET HEALTHCARE.**

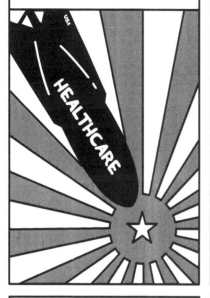

THE WAR ON FREE MARKET HEALTHCARE REVOLVES AROUND GOVERNMENT TAKING OVER HEALTHCARE UNDER THE GUISE THAT HEALTHCARE SHOULD BE A RIGHT OF ALL CITIZENS OF A COUNTRY AND THAT POOR PEOPLE SHOULD HAVE THE SAME HEALTHCARE AS THE WEALTHY.

IT'S A GREAT GOVERNMENT LIE. BUT THE REALITY IS THAT HEALTHCARE COSTS MONEY AND NOT ALL HEALTHCARE IS EQUAL. THEREFORE, A TIER-LESS HEALTH SYSTEM IS A **PIPE** DREAM.

THE TREACHERY OF GOVERNMENT FIXES

This is not a formula for fair healthcare

IN AN EFFORT TO MAKE A TIER-LESS HEALTH SYSTEM, GOVERNMENTS NEED TO MAKE INFORMATION ILLEGAL ABOUT WHAT DOCTORS ARE BEST. BECAUSE PEOPLE WANT TO GO TO WHOEVER IS THE BEST. THAT'S WHY THE BEST USUALLY COSTS THE MOST. [1]

THE END RESULT IS STILL A TIERED SYSTEM. AT THE TOP ARE POLITICIANS AND MEDIA PUNDITS WHO ARE GIVEN GREAT TREATMENT SO THEY CAN GO ON PUBLICLY ABOUT HOW GREAT THEIR EXPERIENCE WITH THE SYSTEM HAS BEEN.

OUR STATE HEALTHCARE SYSTEM IS WONDERFUL!

NEXT ARE MEDICAL INSIDERS WHO HAVE ACCESS TO THE INFORMATION MADE ILLEGAL. THEN THERE ARE PEOPLE WEALTHY ENOUGH TO FLY TO FREER HEALTH SYSTEMS. AND AT THE BOTTOM IS EVERYONE ELSE.

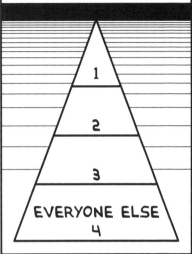

1

2

3

EVERYONE ELSE
4

EVEN WHERE HEALTHCARE IS SUPPOSEDLY PRIVATE, IT IS STILL HEAVILY REGULATED AND HEAVILY DISTORTED BY GOVERNMENT. HAVE YOU EVER GONE INTO A HOSPITAL IN THE U.S. AND NOTICED A BOARD WITH ALL THE PRICES OF SERVICES ON IT?

5 MINUTES WITH A DOCTOR: TOTAL RIP-OFF

BLOOD WORK: WAY MORE THAN BLOOD IS WORTH

SURGERY: YOU'LL WISH YOU HAD DIED

OUTPATIENT PROCEDURE: WE'LL SEE, BUT REST ASSURED IT WILL BE BAD

OVERNIGHT STAY: THE RITZ CARLTON IS CHEAPER AND MUCH NICER

IF THE GOVERNMENT DOESN'T MAKE PEOPLE DIRECTLY DEPENDENT ON ITSELF FOR HEALTHCARE, THEN IT DOES THINGS LIKE USE THE TAX LAWS TO MAKE PEOPLE DIRECTLY DEPENDENT ON EMPLOYER PROVIDED HEALTH BENEFITS.

THE RESULT IS A CORPORATIST SYSTEM WHERE REGULAR FREE MARKET FORCES THAT KEEP COSTS IN CHECK NO LONGER APPLY.

PAYMENTS ARE MADE BY THIRD PARTIES (LIKE CORPORATIST INSURANCE COMPANIES AND GOVERNMENT HEALTH INSURANCE/BENEFIT SYSTEMS), NOT THE PEOPLE GETTING THE MEDICAL CARE.

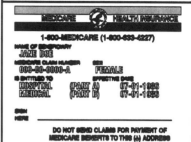

THEN THERE IS ALSO THE FACTOR OF PATIENTS TOO OFTEN USING THE GUNS OF GOVERNMENT TO SUE DOCTORS FOR MALPRACTICE. IN A FREE SYSTEM, LIABILITY WOULD BE LIMITED AND LIKELY SPELLED OUT IN A PATIENT–DOCTOR CONTRACT.

IT'S NO SURPRISE GOVERNMENT IS SO INTERESTED IN HEALTHCARE THOUGH. ONCE GOVERNMENT CAN GET CITIZENRY THINKING THAT HEALTHCARE CAN'T EXIST WITHOUT GOVERNMENT, GOVERNMENT HAS SUCCEEDED IN A MAJOR POWER GRAB.

THE WAR ON DRUGS IS ANOTHER EXAMPLE OF THE HEALTH AND GROWTH OF GOVERNMENT THROUGH WAR.

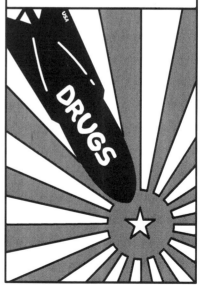

ANYTHING THAT IS MADE ILLEGAL CREATES A BLACK MARKET. AND THE PROBLEM WITH A BLACK MARKET IS THAT IT IS A HIDDEN MARKET. A HIDDEN MARKET LACKS THE TRANSPARENCY OF A FREE MARKET AND THUS A HIDDEN MARKET LACKS SOME OF THE FEEDBACK MECHANISMS THAT LEAD TO THE HONEST, VOLUNTARY EXCHANGE OF GOODS AND SERVICES.

IF YOU'RE SELLING DRUGS AND DRUGS ARE ILLEGAL, THEN, UNLIKE IF YOU WERE DEALING IN A FREE MARKET, YOUR CLIENT HAS AN INCENTIVE TO SIMPLY BEAT YOU UP AND STEAL THE DRUGS.

IF YOU WERE BEAT UP AND HAD YOUR DRUGS STOLEN FROM YOU, YOU WOULDN'T GO AROUND AND MAKE IT VERY PUBLIC THAT THIS CLIENT STOLE DRUGS FROM YOU. THAT IS BECAUSE IF YOU MADE IT TOO PUBLIC, THE COPS WOULD FIND OUT THAT YOU'RE A DRUG DEALER.

IN A FREE MARKET, HONESTY, PEACE, AND TRANSPARENCY ARE THE MOST PROFITABLE. BUT IN A BLACK MARKET, DISHONESTY, FORCE, AND SECRECY BECOME PROFITABLE TOO.

THEREFORE, THE WAR ON DRUGS CREATES A CRIMINAL CLASS OF PEOPLE TO JUSTIFY A STRONGER, BIGGER GOVERNMENT IN THE FORM OF POLICE.

AND THAT CRIMINAL CLASS IS ENDLESSLY HYPED THROUGH PROPAGANDA LIKE NEWS AND CRIME DRAMAS.

THE SIMPLETON RUSE OF PAINTING THE WAR ON DRUGS AS A WAY TO KEEP KIDS OFF DRUGS DOESN'T STOP DRUG USE IN AS MUCH AS IT SIMPLY PUSHES IT UNDERGROUND LEADING TO CRIMINAL ACTIVITY, LIKE GANGS...AND CRIMINAL ACTIVITY LIKE THEFT BY JUNKIES NEEDING FUNDS TO SUPPORT THEIR ARTIFICIALLY COSTLY HABIT.

A WAR ON DRUGS IS THE KIND OF INSANE THING THAT ONLY GOVERNMENT COULD GET AWAY WITH. IF PRIVATE CITIZENS HAD TO FUND A WAR ON DRUGS VOLUNTARILY, IT WOULDN'T GET VERY FAR.

NOT ONLY IS A WAR ON DRUGS DUMB IN THE SENSE THAT IT CREATES CRIMINALITY, BUT IT IS ALSO DUMB IN WHAT IT DEEMS AS LEGAL AND ILLEGAL DRUGS. FOR INSTANCE, IN MANY PLACES WHERE MARIJUANA IS ILLEGAL, ALCOHOL IS PERFECTLY LEGAL.

SPEND A DAY WITH A POTHEAD SOMETIME AND THEN SPEND A DAY WITH A DRUNK. ALSO, LET A POTHEAD DRIVE YOU AROUND AND THEN LET A DRUNK. IF YOU ARE STILL ALIVE, TELL ME WHICH DRUG IS MORE PROBLEMATIC, MARIJUANA OR ALCOHOL?

THE FACT IS THAT MOST OF THE PEOPLE AGAINST MOST DRUGS DON'T KNOW WHAT THEY ARE EVEN AGAINST. BECAUSE THEY HAVE NO FIRSTHAND EXPERIENCE OF TAKING ALL THE DRUGS THEY ARE AGAINST TO FIND OUT WHAT THEY ARE REALLY LIKE. IT IS LIKE DEAF PEOPLE CRITIQUING MUSIC.

THE PERCEPTION OF MOST DRUGS IS JUST A PRODUCT OF BLIND CULTURAL BIAS. CAFFEINE IS A DRUG. BUT SINCE IT IS A DRUG COMPATIBLE WITH BEING A GOOD, EFFICIENT ROBOT (SPINNING THE GEARS OF THE SOCIOECONOMIC MACHINERY ON THE TAX FARM) CAFFEINE IS UBIQUITOUS.

74

THE REALITY IS THAT PEOPLE BOUND AND DETERMINED TO RUIN THEMSELVES WITH DRUGS AREN'T GOING TO LET GOVERNMENT ILLEGALIZATION GET IN THE WAY, NOR IS LEGALIZATION GOING TO TURN PEOPLE UNINTERESTED IN DRUGS INTO DRUG ADDICTS.

ALL A MORE OBEDIENT SELF-DESTRUCTIVE PERSON WILL DO IS FIND LEGAL DRUGS TO ABUSE, LIKE ALCOHOL AND PRESCRIPTIONS.

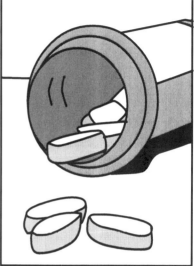

WHICH BRINGS UP ANOTHER POINT: THE WAR ON DRUGS, LIKE ALL GOVERNMENT WARS, ALSO INCLUDES AN UNHEALTHY DOSE OF CORPORATISM. IT SUPPRESSES USEFUL CROPS LIKE HEMP.

PLUS, IT KEEPS THE CHEAP AND EASY DRUGS THAT YOU COULD GROW IN YOUR BACK YARD OFF THE MARKET IN EXCHANGE FOR THINGS LIKE PATENTED PRESCRIPTION DRUGS.

COCAINE, HEROIN, OPIUM, MORPHINE... IN MY DAY, WE CALLED THAT MEDICINE!

75

PATENTS ARE A PRIME EXAMPLE OF A COERCIVE MONOPOLISTIC PRIVILEGE GRANTED BY THE GOVERNMENT. IF YOU WANTED TO KEEP INFORMATION SECRET IN A FREE SOCIETY, YOU WOULD BE RESPONSIBLE FOR DOING SO YOURSELF WITHOUT THE THREAT OF FORCE.

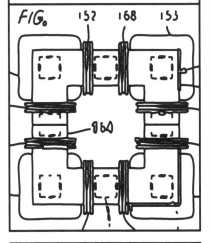

PATENTS ARE AN ARTIFICIAL PERK FOR BUSINESSES MADE POSSIBLE BY GOVERNMENT, WHICH WE'LL EXPLORE IN MORE DETAIL LATER. ANOTHER ARTIFICIAL PERK FOR BUSINESSES MADE POSSIBLE BY GOVERNMENT IS THE ABILITY TO POLLUTE.

THUS, ANOTHER GOVERNMENT WAR COULD BE DESCRIBED AS **THE WAR ON POLLUTION**.

IT IS A TESTAMENT TO THE EFFECTIVENESS OF GOVERNMENT PROPAGANDA THAT SO FEW PEOPLE ARE AWARE THAT POLLUTION IS A PROBLEM WHICH PRIMARILY STEMS FROM GOVERNMENT. AFTER ALL, HAVE YOU EVER SEEN THE ENVIRONMENTAL DEGRADATION OF WARS?

POLLUTION IS A PROPERTY RIGHTS ISSUE. POLLUTION IS A FORM OF THE INITIATION OF FORCE. IF YOU ARE DOWNWIND OF SOMEONE BURNING GARBAGE, THEN THAT IS REALLY NO DIFFERENT THAN THE GARBAGE BURNER GOING UP TO YOU AND SPITTING IN YOUR FACE. THE SAME APPLIES TO ALL POLLUTION.

IF SOME TEEN RIDES THROUGH YOUR NEIGHBORHOOD WITH HIS CAR SOUND SYSTEM BLARING BASS AT TWO IN THE MORNING AWAKENING YOU FROM SLEEP, THAT NOISE POLLUTION IS EQUIVALENT TO THAT PERSON COMING INTO YOUR ROOM AND FLICKING YOUR EAR TO WAKE YOU UP. IT'S A FORM OF THE INITIATION OF FORCE.

I'D LIKE TO LAUNCH A GRENADE AT THAT DOUCHE BAG'S CAR.

BOOM BOOM BOOM

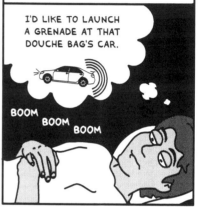

THE PREVALENCE OF THAT KIND OF UBIQUITOUS POLLUTION IN SOCIETY IS SYMPTOMATIC OF A KIND OF VIOLENCE THAT LACKS RESPECT FOR PRIVATE PROPERTY. IT IS POLLUTION SOCIALISM.

OBVIOUSLY, NO MAN IS AN ISLAND, AND JUST BEING IN THE SAME ROOM WITH ANOTHER PERSON MEANS BREATHING IN THE SAME AIR AND THUS BEING POLLUTED BY THE OTHER PERSON'S GERMS. THEREFORE, YOU DON'T WANT TO GET TOO CARRIED AWAY WITH THE POLLUTION IDEA.

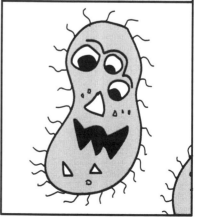

NONETHELESS, WE SHOULD ALL HAVE THE RIGHT TO POLLUTION TOLERANCES OF OUR OWN DETERMINATION. POLLUTION SHOULD BE VOLUNTARY. AND IN A FREE, VOLUNTARYIST SOCIETY, POLLUTION WOULD BE VOLUNTARY. THERE WOULD BE NEAR ZERO POLLUTION TOLERANCE FOR POLLUTING OTHER PEOPLE'S PROPERTY, INCLUDING THE COMMONS LIKE AIR AND WATER.

THAT WOULD MEAN PEOPLE WOULD BE REQUIRED TO TIGHTLY CONTAIN POLLUTION TO THEIR OWN PROPERTY. ALL PRODUCTS WOULD THUS CARRY WITH THEM THE COST OF CONTAINING POLLUTION--INSTEAD OF SOCIALIZING POLLUTION, WHICH IS WHAT HAPPENS IN A GOVERNMENT SOCIETY.

OBVIOUSLY, THINGS LIKE COAL-BURNING POWER PLANTS AND GASOLINE-POWERED CARS ARE PRODUCTS OF THE SOCIALIZATION OF POLLUTION. IN ORDER TO CONTAIN POLLUTION, SUCH THINGS WOULD LIKELY BE MUCH DIFFERENT IN A VOLUNTARYIST SOCIETY.

AS LONG AS GOVERNMENT DEEMS CERTAIN POLLUTION ACCEPTABLE, YOU'VE GOT NO CHOICE BUT TO DEAL WITH IT.

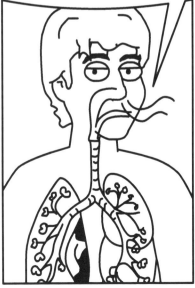

AND WHEN GOVERNMENT DECIDES TO FIGHT POLLUTION, YOU JUST KNOW THAT POLLUTION ISN'T GOING ANYWHERE FOR AS LONG AS IT CAN BE USED TO WAGE WAR.

IN RECENT HISTORY, THE IDEA OF MANMADE CLIMATE CHANGE IS SOMETHING THAT SOME GOVERNMENTS HAVE LATCHED ONTO AS A BATTLE CRY IN THE WAR AGAINST POLLUTION.

a convenient excuse for a power grab

WHETHER MANMADE CLIMATE CHANGE IS TRUE OR NOT WOULDN'T MATTER IN A VOLUNTARYIST SOCIETY, BECAUSE POLLUTION WOULD BE KEPT IN CHECK ANYWAY.

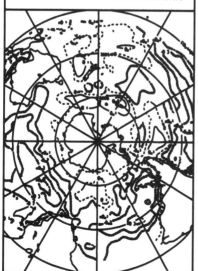

BUT IN THE GOVERNMENT WORLD, AN IDEA LIKE MANMADE CLIMATE CHANGE BECOMES AN EXCUSE FOR GROWTH OF GOVERNMENT, WHICH MEANS MANMADE CLIMATE CHANGE IS GOOD. THEREFORE, GOVERNMENTS EAGER TO WAGE WAR ARE HAPPY TO FUND SCIENTISTS THAT WILL COME TO CONCLUSIONS THEY WANT TO HEAR.

79

TO QUELL CLIMATE CHANGE, GOVERNMENTS DO THINGS LIKE PROPOSE TAXING POLLUTION AS A SOLUTION, WHICH IS A GOOD IDEA ONLY IF YOUR GOAL IS TO GROW GOVERNMENT. IT IS A LAME IDEA THOUGH IF YOU WANT TO STOP POLLUTION.

IF YOU WANT TO STOP POLLUTION, PROTECT PROPERTY RIGHTS. AND THE BEST WAY TO DO THAT IS TO DISSOLVE GOVERNMENT AND REPLACE IT WITH VOLUNTARYISM.

MOST PEOPLE AUTOMATICALLY THINK, IN TANDEM WITH THEIR GOVERNMENT CONDITIONING, THAT WITHOUT A GOVERNMENT, BUSINESSES WOULD POLLUTE WITHOUT RESTRAINT AND DESTROY THE WORLD.
THAT IS COMPLETELY WRONG.

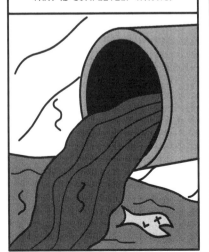

THE REASON BUSINESSES POLLUTE AT ALL TODAY IS A RESULT OF THE GOVERNMENT; PARTICULARLY, AS A RESULT OF THE GOVERNMENT CREATED PHANTOM KNOWN AS THE CORPORATION.

A CORPORATION IS A LEGAL FICTION THAT TRANSFERS LIABILITY FROM THE PEOPLE WHO RUN AND OWN THE CORPORATION TO THE CORPORATION ITSELF. THAT MEANS THE PEOPLE WHO RUN AND OWN THE CORPORATION GET TO REAP ALL THE GAINS WHILE THE FICTIONAL CORPORATION DEALS WITH THE LOSSES AND LIABILITIES. IT'S LIKE BEING ABLE TO ROB A BANK WITH A SOCK PUPPET AND ONLY THE SOCK PUPPET CAN GET IN TROUBLE.

SO, TAKE AN OIL CORPORATION AS AN EXAMPLE OF A BUSINESS MADE POSSIBLE BY INCORPORATION. DRILLING FOR OIL CAN BE A RISKY, DIRTY, POLLUTING BUSINESS.

THEREFORE, IF THE INDIVIDUALS IN AN OIL COMPANY WERE ON THE HOOK FINANCIALLY AND LEGALLY FOR SOMETHING LIKE AN OIL SPILL, OIL WOULD LIKELY BE A MUCH LESS VITAL PART OF THE ECONOMY.

THE TRUE COST OF DRILLING, TRANSPORTING, AND EVEN BURNING OIL WOULD BE FACTORED INTO ITS COST, THUS MAKING ALTERNATIVES MORE APPEALING AND ECONOMICALLY VIABLE.

IN A TRUE FREE MARKET, WITH GREED COMES FEAR. GREED MEANS RISK AND RISK IS SCARY WHEN YOU PERSONALLY HAVE TO PAY THE PRICE WHEN THINGS GO WRONG. INCORPORATION RUINS THAT FEEDBACK MECHANISM. AND GOVERNMENT BAILOUTS RUIN THAT FEEDBACK MECHANISM TOO.

THAT'S WHY ALL YOU SINCERE ENVIRONMENTALISTS LOOKING TO GOVERNMENT TO SAVE THE ENVIRONMENT NEED TO START THINKING OUTSIDE THE BOX OF GOVERNMENT PROPAGANDA.

YOU CAN'T REALLY GET RID OF INCORPORATION WITHOUT GETTING RID OF GOVERNMENT. AS LONG AS GOVERNMENT GUNS CAN BE USED AGAINST BUSINESSES, SUCH AS THROUGH THINGS LIKE FRIVOLOUS LAWSUITS, BUSINESSES ARE NATURALLY GOING TO WANT TO UTILIZE GOVERNMENT GUNS THEMSELVES FOR PROTECTION.

IN A VOLUNTARYIST SOCIETY, MAKING MONEY WOULD BE CONTINGENT ON MAINTAINING A GOOD REPUTATION BY STAYING TRUE TO THE PRINCIPLES OF VOLUNTARYISM. AND PEOPLE WHO TRIED TO VIOLATE THE PRINCIPLES OF VOLUNTARYISM WOULD BE OSTRACIZED AND THUS FINANCIALLY LIMITED.

THE FINAL TYPE OF GOVERNMENT WAR WE SHOULD LOOK AT IS WHAT COULD BE CALLED **THE VOTING WAR**.

THIS PARTICULAR GOVERNMENT WAR IS A WAR BETWEEN THE SLAVES OVER HOW THE MASTER SHOULD RUN THE PLANTATION.

IMPLICIT IN THE VOTING WAR IS THE ACCEPTANCE THAT THE GOVERNMENT DOES AND SHOULD EXIST. THEREFORE, EVEN WHEN SMALL GOVERNMENT PEOPLE, LIKE LIBERTARIANS, PARTICIPATE IN THE VOTING WAR, THEY ARE STILL HELPING THE HEALTH OF THE GOVERNMENT.

A VOLUNTARYIST SOCIETY IS NOT GOING TO ARISE FROM VOTING. VOTING IS FOR SLAVES. VOTING IS THE SLAVE SUGGESTION BOX AS I'VE ALREADY ALLUDED TO.

VOTE FOR NO ONE!

* NO ONE WILL STOP ALL THE WARS.
* NO ONE WILL REFORM THE MONETARY SYSTEM.
* NO ONE WILL END THE DEBT.
* NO ONE WILL FIX THE ECONOMY.
* NO ONE WILL MAKE YOU FREE.
* NO ONE SHARES YOUR IDEAL FOR HOW YOU SHOULD LIVE YOUR LIFE.

YOU CAN'T APPEAL TO YOUR MASTER FOR FREEDOM. THE MERE APPEAL REINFORCES THE SLAVE MASTER HIERARCHY.

THE MASTER IS A GHOST THAT IS MADE REAL BY ACKNOWLEDGING IT; IT IS A FICTITIOUS HIERARCHY THAT DISAPPEARS WHEN THE SLAVES STOP PLAYING THE ROLE OF SLAVES.

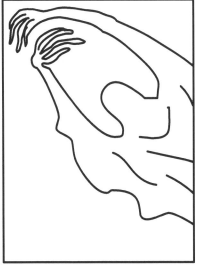

THE FREER YOU ARE THE LESS SENSE VOTING MAKES. IF YOU ARE A WAGE SLAVE, OR SOME OTHER SLAVE VARIANT, GO AHEAD AND VOTE IF THAT STUFF MATTERS TO YOU. BUT I'D PERSONALLY SPEND MY TIME ON MAKING MYSELF MORE FREE SO AS NOT TO BE DEPENDENT ON THE GOVERNMENT TO BEGIN WITH.

A SHINING EXAMPLE OF A SLAVE VOTING WAR HAS BEEN THE AMERICAN SAME-SEX MARRIAGE WAR BETWEEN THOSE WHO WANT SAME-SEX COUPLES TO HAVE THE SAME RIGHTS AS HETEROSEXUAL MARRIED COUPLES AND THOSE WHO DO NOT.

MARRIAGE WAR

THE REALITY IS THAT GOVERNMENT SHOULD HAVE NOTHING TO DO WITH ANYTHING PERIOD, LET ALONE MARRIAGE, STRAIGHT OR GAY.

84

MARRIAGE IS A PRIVATE CONTRACT BETWEEN CONSENTING ADULTS THAT REQUIRES NO GOVERNMENT.

THE FACT THAT PEOPLE THINK THEY NEED AN IMAGINARY THING CALLED GOVERNMENT TO WAVE A MAGIC WAND TO MAKE A MARRIAGE REAL IS JUST A SIGN OF THEIR ENSLAVEMENT. ONLY A SLAVE SAYS:

MASTER, MASTER, PLEASE LET ME DO WHAT IS VOLUNTARY.

INSTEAD YOU SAY:

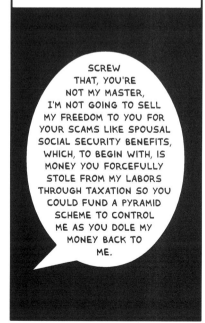

SCREW THAT, YOU'RE NOT MY MASTER, I'M NOT GOING TO SELL MY FREEDOM TO YOU FOR YOUR SCAMS LIKE SPOUSAL SOCIAL SECURITY BENEFITS, WHICH, TO BEGIN WITH, IS MONEY YOU FORCEFULLY STOLE FROM MY LABORS THROUGH TAXATION SO YOU COULD FUND A PYRAMID SCHEME TO CONTROL ME AS YOU DOLE MY MONEY BACK TO ME.

WHEN GAYS FIGHT FOR THE RIGHT TO MARRY, THEY ARE MERELY REINFORCING THE VERY GOVERNMENTAL SYSTEM OF FORCE THAT EVER MADE GAY MARRIAGE ILLEGAL IN THE FIRST PLACE. IT'S SLAVE PROTEST.

AND WHEN PEOPLE OF EVERY VARIETY, NAMELY THE RELIGIOUS VARIETY, FIGHT TO KEEP MARRIAGE STRICTLY BETWEEN A MAN AND A WOMAN, THEY ARE MERELY REINFORCING THE VERY GOVERNMENTAL SYSTEM THAT ALREADY LIMITS THEIR OWN RIGHTS.

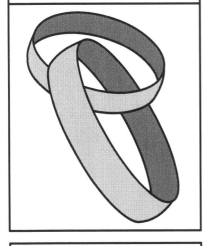

GOVERNMENT'S INVOLVEMENT IN MARRIAGE WAS HISTORICALLY USED TO PREVENT THINGS LIKE INTERRACIAL MARRIAGES AND TO ENTICE WOMEN TO GET MARRIED BY OFFERING THEM SPECIAL RIGHTS THEY SHOULD HAVE HAD TO BEGIN WITH, LIKE THE RIGHT OF PROPERTY OWNERSHIP.

GOVERNMENT MARRIAGE IS ABOUT CONTROLLING PEOPLE AND LIMITING FREEDOM, NOT EXPANDING IT. THE MAIN REASON THAT NOT BEING MARRIED BY GOVERNMENT IS A PROBLEM IS BECAUSE IN A GOVERNMENT SOCIETY RIGHTS ARE LIMITED.

FOR INSTANCE, YOU DON'T REALLY OWN YOUR OWN STUFF. YOU CAN'T PASS ON YOUR OWN PROPERTY WITHOUT GOVERNMENT LOOKING OVER IT TO SEE WHAT CUT IT CAN STEAL.

YOU SHOULD BE ABLE TO PASS ON YOUR PROPERTY TO ANYONE WITHOUT ANY GOVERNMENT INVOLVEMENT.

TECHNICALLY, YOU CAN IF YOU DO IT UNDER THE TABLE, BUT THAT'S HARD TO DO WHEN YOU NEED TO PASS ON OWNERSHIP OF A HOUSE AFTER SOMEONE HAS UNEXPECTEDLY DIED. A HOUSE IS, AFTER ALL, USUALLY RENTED FROM THE GOVERNMENT THROUGH PROPERTY TAX.

IN A FREE SOCIETY, YOU COULD WRITE UP ANY CONTRACT WITH ANYONE YOU WANT TO DO ANYTHING. YOU WOULDN'T NEED SPECIAL RIGHTS FROM THE GOVERNMENT IN THE FORM OF A SANCTIFIED MARRIAGE.

SO, INSTEAD OF ASKING FOR RIGHTS, PEOPLE SHOULD BE AGAINST ALL THE STUFF LIMITING THEIR RIGHTS IN THE FIRST PLACE.

MEET THE PRESS TITUTES

KEEP THOSE CAMPAIGN ADVERTISING DOLLARS COMING OUR WAY AND WE'LL DO WHATEVER YOU WANT.

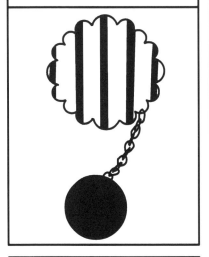

THAT'S THE REALITY, BUT THAT'S NEVER PART OF THE MAINSTREAM DIALOGUE, BECAUSE THE SLAVES WERE NOT TAUGHT TO THINK FREELY. CONSEQUENTLY, THEY DON'T THINK LIKE THAT; THEY THINK LIKE PRISONERS.

THE SLAVES ARE MOSTLY JUST CONCERNED ABOUT HOW THE GOVERNMENT IS GOING TO DOLE OUT ALL THE DEBT AND TAXATION.

BUT ANYWAY, THAT'S ENOUGH ON GOVERNMENT WARS. YOU SHOULD GET THE POINT.

NEXT WE ARE GOING TO LOOK AT CORPORATISM VERSUS CUSTOMERISM.

CHAPTER FOUR

CORPORATISM VERSUS CUSTOMERISM

AS I ALREADY MENTIONED, THERE IS NO FREE MARKET WITHOUT FREE MARKET MONEY. THEREFORE, EVEN ON THE MOST BASIC LEVEL, BUSINESSES IN THE CONTEMPORARY WORLD DON'T OPERATE IN A FREE MARKET.

CURRENCY SUPPLY AND INTEREST RATES ARE CENTRALLY CONTROLLED BY GOVERNMENT-SANCTIONED CENTRAL BANKS.

BUT GOVERNMENT DOES A LOT MORE TO SCREW UP FREE MARKET FORCES THAN JUST THROUGH ITS COMPLACENCY WITH DEBT CURRENCY SCHEMES. INCORPORATION, FOR EXAMPLE, GREATLY SCREWS UP FREE MARKET FORCES.

IN GENERAL, WHEN GOVERNMENT MERGES WITH BUSINESS, GOVERNMENT GIVES BUSINESS A BAD NAME. PEOPLE THINK THAT WHAT BUSINESS IS IN A GOVERNMENT WORLD IS THE SAME AS WHAT BUSINESS IS IN A FREE WORLD.

WHAT BUSINESS IS IN A GOVERNMENT-HAUNTED WORLD IS CORPORATISM; IT IS NOT A FREE MARKET.

WHEN YOU GIVE AN ENTITY A MONOPOLY ON FORCE, YOU CAN'T BLAME BUSINESSES TOO MUCH FOR WANTING TO USE THE GUN IN THE ROOM TO MAKE MONEY, BECAUSE IF THEY DON'T, THEIR COMPETITORS WILL. SO, IT IS ONLY NATURAL.

AND IT ISN'T JUST BUSINESSES THAT TRY TO USE THE GUNS, THINGS LIKE LABOR UNIONS TRY TO USE GOVERNMENT GUNS TOO, ESPECIALLY PUBLIC SECTOR UNIONS; AS IF A UNION FOR PEOPLE WHOSE PAYCHECKS ARE FUNDED BY TAXES (THEFT) MAKES ANY SENSE.

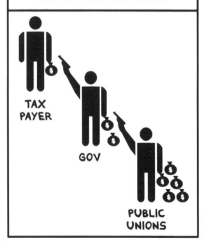

TAX PAYER

GOV

PUBLIC UNIONS

A BUSINESS DEPENDENT ON POLITICAL CONNIVING IS A CORRUPT BUSINESS. AND SADLY, A CORRUPT BUSINESS ALMOST ALWAYS BECOMES DISTORTED IN PUBLIC PERCEPTION AS PROOF OF WHY WE NEED GOVERNMENT TO REGULATE BUSINESS.

BUT THAT IS COMPLETELY WRONG SINCE GOVERNMENT IS THE CORRUPTING ELEMENT TO BEGIN WITH. WHEN GOVERNMENT WAGES WAR ON CORRUPT BUSINESS, IT IS REALLY A WAR ON ITSELF. BUT IT IS NEVER FORMULATED TRUTHFULLY LIKE THAT.

GOVERNMENT HAS THE GUN, BUSINESSES DON'T. GIVING GOVERNMENT MORE POWER OVER BUSINESSES JUST MAKES BUSINESSES MORE COZY WITH GOVERNMENT AND THE GUN OF GOVERNMENT IS THUS USED IN BUSINESS.

THE BUSINESSES THAT AREN'T COZY WITH AND SUBSIDIZED BY GOVERNMENT HAVE TO COMPETE WITH THOSE THAT ARE.

THE ADVANTAGE OF RUNNING AN HONEST BUSINESS FREE OF GOVERNMENT PERKS IS THAT MANY OF THE FEEDBACK MECHANISMS NEEDED TO MAXIMIZE EFFICIENCY AND QUALITY STAY IN PLACE. THAT MAKES FOR THE BEST, MOST DESIRABLE PRODUCT FOR LONG-TERM SUSTAINABILITY.

LEGITIMATE BUSINESSES OPERATE WITHIN THE RULES OF WHAT IS BEST DESCRIBED AS **CUSTOMERISM:** MAKE THE CUSTOMER HAPPY BECAUSE THAT IS WHERE ALL THE PROFIT IS, NOT IN GOVERNMENT SUBSIDIES, OR SPECIAL TAX BREAKS, OR PATENT TROLLING, OR AN INFLATED STOCK PRICE, OR BRINGING ANTI-TRUST SUITS AGAINST SUCCESSFUL COMPETITORS.

CUSTOMERISM IS WHAT REIGNS IN A FREE, VOLUNTARYIST ECONOMY; THERE IS NO OTHER VIABLE OPTION.

PART OF CUSTOMERISM IS NOT ONLY MAKING CUSTOMERS HAPPY BUT ALSO MAKING EMPLOYEES HAPPY. IN A FREE ECONOMY, THERE WOULD BE NO ARTIFICIAL BARRIERS TO ENTRY FOR BUSINESSES AND THUS EMPLOYEES WOULD HAVE PLENTY OF OPTIONS. NO EMPLOYEES, NO PRODUCT, NO CUSTOMERS, NO MONEY.

BUT IN A GOVERNMENT ECONOMY, EVEN POLITICALLY UNCONNECTED BUSINESSES HAVE THE OPTION OF THE GOVERNMENT GIFT OF INCORPORATION. THAT IS SUCH A VALUABLE GIFT (PROTECTION) THAT DESPITE ALL THE CORRUPTION OF GOVERNMENT--ALL THE REGULATION AND TAXATION--BUSINESSES TEND TO JUST PUT UP WITH GOVERNMENT.

THINGS LIKE THE MONOPOLISTIC COERCION MADE POSSIBLE BY PATENTS ARE ALSO APPEALING TO BUSINESSES.

CONSEQUENTLY, MOST BUSINESSES DON'T TALK ABOUT ELIMINATING GOVERNMENT, JUST MAKING IT MORE BUSINESS FRIENDLY.

MR. VOLUNTARY SAYS:

IF VOLUNTARYISM WOULD BENEFIT BIG CORPORATIONS, THEY'D SUPPORT VOLUNTARYISM. BUT THEY SUPPORT CORPORATISM.

THE AVERAGE SLAVE IS AN EMPLOYEE AND NOT AN ENTREPRENEUR. MANY EMPLOYEES DON'T EVEN WORK FOR BUSINESSES, THEY WORK FOR THE GOVERNMENT.

UNIONS MAKE US CORPORATISTS

THE BUREAUCRACY ONE HAS TO GO THROUGH IN A GOVERNMENT ECONOMY TO BE AN ENTREPRENEUR ACTS AS A BARRIER TO ENTRY.

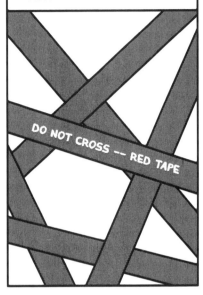

DO NOT CROSS -- RED TAPE

BEING AN EMPLOYEE IS EASIER, SO BEING AN ENTREPRENEUR IS NOT EVEN CONSIDERED BY MOST.

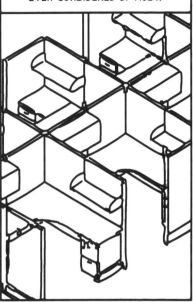

THAT TRANSLATES INTO THE AVERAGE SLAVE BEING FOCUSED ONLY ON THE DEMAND SIDE OF THE ECONOMY AND NOT THE SUPPLY SIDE. THE AVERAGE SLAVE IS A CONSUMER AND NOT A PRODUCER.

I Shop therefore I am

DRAWING OF UNTITLED BY BARBARA KRUGER

THEREFORE, THE AVERAGE SLAVE CARES ONLY ABOUT DEMAND SIDE FREEDOM AND NOT SUPPLY SIDE FREEDOM, WHICH IS A PERFECT RECIPE FOR A CORPORATIST SOCIETY WITH AN ECONOMY DOMINATED BY LARGE BUSINESSES THAT ARE IN CAHOOTS WITH GOVERNMENT.

Inc.

AND CORPORATIST SOCIETIES SCALE DOWN TOO, BECAUSE THERE IS ALSO PLENTY OF CORPORATISM ON THE LOCAL GOVERNMENT LEVEL, WHICH HELPS CERTAIN BUSINESSES DOMINATE LOCALLY.

DEMAND SIDE VERSUS SUPPLY SIDE FREEDOM REALLY SAYS A LOT ABOUT THE CONTEMPORARY GOVERNMENT ECONOMIC SYSTEM.

THE CONTEMPORARY GOVERNMENT ECONOMIC SYSTEM IS DOMINATED BY THE DEMAND SIDE; THAT'S REALLY ALL MOST PEOPLE CARE ABOUT. THE CHOICE OF COKE VERSUS PEPSI IS A CLASSIC EXAMPLE OF DEMAND SIDE FREEDOM.

BUT THE SUPPLY SIDE IS NOT VERY FREE IN THE GOVERNMENT SYSTEM. THE SYSTEM IS QUITE DISCOURAGING UNLESS YOU HAVE SOME VARIANT OF OBSESSIVE COMPULSIVE DISORDER AND GET OFF ON FOLLOWING POINTLESS RULES, OR YOU LIKE TO WORK HARD TO KEEP TRACK OF MONEY SO YOU CAN GIVE IT TO THE GOVERNMENT TO PISS AWAY ON THE POLITICALLY CONNECTED.

THE GOVERNMENT SYSTEM IS UNFRIENDLY TO SMALL PLAYERS TRYING TO ENTER THE SUPPLY SIDE ARENA, WHICH LIMITS COMPETITION AND THUS GIVES AN UNFAIR ADVANTAGE TO BOTH THE SUPPLY SIDE PLAYERS ALREADY DOCTORED INTO THE SYSTEM AND TO PLAYERS WITH THE ECONOMIES OF SCALE NEEDED TO COMPLY WITH GOVERNMENT. IT'S A SYSTEM OF BIG BUSINESS IN CAHOOTS WITH BIG GOVERNMENT; IT IS CORPORATISM.

POLITICS ALSO NATURALLY FOLLOWS THE DEMAND SIDE DYNAMIC. JUST LIKE COKE AND PEPSI, IN THE UNITED STATES, THERE ARE THE REPUBLICANS AND DEMOCRATS; THEY EVEN USE THE SAME DIFFERENTIATING COLORS AS COKE AND PEPSI.

THE SUPPLY SIDE OF UNITED STATES POLITICS IS EVEN MORE LIMITING THAN THE SUPPLY SIDE OF CORPORATIST GOODS AND SERVICES. THIRD PARTIES AND INDEPENDENTS JUST CAN'T COMPETE WITH THE REPS AND DEMS WHO ESTABLISH THE EDGES OF ACCEPTABLE POLITICAL VIEWS.

THIRD PARTIES HAVE A HARD TIME GETTING ON THE BALLOT, A HARD TIME GETTING CORPORATE MEDIA COVERAGE, AND A HARD TIME GETTING SUPPORT FROM VOTERS. OVERALL, WHAT THE REPS AND DEMS GIVE IS THAT WHICH APPEASES AND PERPETUATES THE DEMAND SIDE SLAVES. AND WHAT APPEASES AND PERPETUATES THE DEMAND SIDE SLAVES IS CORPORATISM.

96

A CORPORATIST SOCIETY DOESN'T REALLY CARE ABOUT THE SUPPLY SIDE. THE PEOPLE OF A CORPORATIST SOCIETY JUST FIND A NICHE WITHIN THE DEMAND SIDE CHOICE OF CORPORATE OR GOVERNMENT EMPLOYMENT.

AND AS A RESULT, THE SLAVES NEVER REALLY HAVE TO DEAL WITH THE FULL SCALE OF THE SUPPLY SIDE OF THE SYSTEM. THEREFORE, THEY DON'T BECOME INTERESTED IN TRULY ANTI-CORPORATIST THINGS LIKE VOLUNTARYISM AND ENDING THE LEGAL FICTION CALLED THE CORPORATION.

INSTEAD, THE SLAVES TAKE THE BAIT AND RAIL AGAINST CORPORATISM BY TRYING TO MAKE GOVERNMENT BIGGER.

WE NEED TO REGULATE BUSINESS.

SO, IT MUST BE EMPHASIZED THAT UNDERSTANDING THE DIFFERENCE BETWEEN CUSTOMERISM AND CORPORATISM IS ESSENTIAL TO BREAKING OUT OF GOVERNMENT ENSLAVEMENT ON AN INTELLECTUAL LEVEL.

CUSTOMERISM:
A NETWORK OF FREE AND VOLUNTARY EXCHANGES IN WHICH PRODUCERS WORK, PRODUCE, AND EXCHANGE THEIR PRODUCTS FOR THE PRODUCTS OF OTHERS THROUGH PRICES VOLUNTARILY ARRIVED AT.

CORPORATISM:
CONSISTS OF ONE OR MORE GROUPS MAKING USE OF THE COERCIVE APPARATUS OF THE GOVERNMENT FOR THEMSELVES BY EXPROPRIATING THE PRODUCTION OF OTHERS BY FORCE AND VIOLENCE. "

THAT SAYS IT ALL. BUSINESSES RELY ON VOLUNTARY EXCHANGE. ONLY IN A WORLD WHERE BUSINESSES CO-EXIST WITH GOVERNMENT DO BUSINESSES HAVE GUNS.

YOU COULDN'T GET AWAY WITH HOLDING A GUN TO THE HEADS OF CUSTOMERS DEMANDING THEY BUY YOUR PRODUCT. BUT THE GOVERNMENT CAN HOLD A GUN TO YOUR HEAD AND MAKE YOU DO ALL KINDS OF THINGS UNDER THE GUISE THAT IT IS THE WILL OF THE PEOPLE.

Chance

THE INSURANCE COMPANIES, IN COLLUSION WITH THE BANKS, JUST REDID THE GOVERNMENT FLOOD MAP TO INCLUDE YOUR HOUSE IN A FLOOD ZONE.

SINCE YOU HAVE A MORTGAGE ON YOUR HOUSE, YOU MUST PAY FOR FLOOD INSURANCE:

$600

MONOPOLIES RELY ON FORCE.

VOLUNTARYISM RELIES ON PEACE AND THUS WIN-WIN RELATIONSHIPS.

IF I HAVE SOMETHING TO SELL YOU AND YOU WANT TO BUY IT, THAT IS A VOLUNTARY RELATIONSHIP. I WANT YOUR MONEY MORE THAN THE THING I HAVE AND YOU WANT THE THING I HAVE MORE THAN YOUR MONEY.

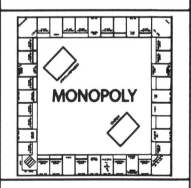

THE GOVERNMENT IS WHAT MAKES THE WORLD LIKE THE GAME MONOPOLY--WHERE YOU HAVE NO CHOICE BUT TO BUY A PARTICULAR PRODUCT.

EVEN IF I WAS SELLING YOU PURE WATER AFTER A NATURAL DISASTER FOR AN EXORBITANT PRICE, THE RELATIONSHIP WOULD STILL BE VOLUNTARY AND WIN-WIN.

PURE WATER $25 PER GALLON

IF YOU ARE WILLING TO PAY AN EXORBITANT PRICE FOR WATER, THEN YOU REALLY WANT IT. AND SINCE I'M THE ONLY ONE WITH WATER TO SELL, I'M GOING TO ALLOCATE IT IN A WAY THAT HONORS ITS SCARCITY.

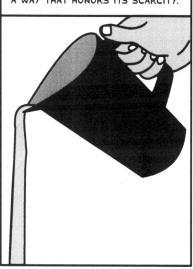

TECHNICALLY, GOVERNMENTS WILL OFTEN ARREST YOU FOR ASSISTING DESPERATE DISASTER SURVIVORS FOR A HEALTHY PROFIT. ONLY GOVERNMENT HELP AND CHARITY ARE ALLOWED.

EVACUATION ROUTE

NEEDLESS TO SAY, THAT IS INCREDIBLY DUMB BECAUSE THE EXTRA HIGH PROFIT MOTIVE IS WHAT WOULD ASSURE THAT THE SCARCITY OF GOODS AND SERVICES CAUSED BY A DISASTER WOULD NOT LAST LONG.

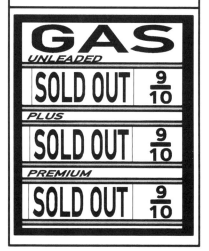

GAS
UNLEADED
SOLD OUT 9/10
PLUS
SOLD OUT 9/10
PREMIUM
SOLD OUT 9/10

YOU SHOULD ALWAYS HAVE THE OPTION OF BREAKING OUT YOUR WALLET TO GET THINGS MOVING NOW INSTEAD OF WAITING FOR SOMETHING LIKE GOVERNMENT OR CHARITY TO HELP YOU.

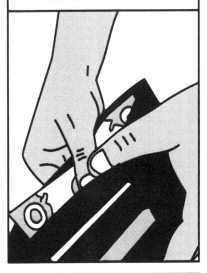

BUT GOVERNMENT SAYS NO, BECAUSE IT'S UNFAIR TO PEOPLE WHO DON'T WANT TO OR CAN'T PAY A PREMIUM.

THAT KIND OF ARTIFICIAL REGULATION RUINS VALUABLE FEEDBACK MECHANISMS. IF PEOPLE KNEW THAT DISASTERS MEANT HIGH PRICES, THEY'D TAKE EXTRA PRECAUTIONS TO BE PREPARED AHEAD OF TIME WHEN PRICES ARE NORMAL.

VOLUNTARY FREE EXCHANGE REWARDS THOSE WHO MAKE THE RIGHT MOVES AND ALLOCATE RESOURCES EFFICIENTLY.

TO HAVE AN EFFICIENT, RESPONSIBLE SOCIETY, YOU NEED THE PROPER FEEDBACK MECHANISMS.

BUT WHETHER IT BE THE LEGAL FICTION THAT IS THE CORPORATION, PRICE GOUGING LAWS, CENTRAL BANKING, OR WHATEVER, THE GOVERNMENT JUST LOVES TO MESS UP THOSE VOLUNTARY FEEDBACK MECHANISMS.

STOP RIGHT THERE VOLUNTARY HUMAN INTERACTION!

THERE'S REALLY NO SCIENCE OF ECONOMICS IN A GOVERNMENT-HAUNTED WORLD ANYMORE THAN THERE WOULD BE A SCIENCE OF PHYSICS IF THE LAWS OF NATURE WERE AT THE WHIM OF PHYSICS LEGISLATORS.

WE NEED TO CHANGE THE SPEED OF LIGHT AND REDUCE THE FORCE OF GRAVITY.

WHICH LEADS US TO ANOTHER THING GOVERNMENT DOES TO MESS UP FREE, VOLUNTARY HUMAN INTERACTION: THE PROTECTION OF INTELLECTUAL PROPERTY.

BY DEFAULT, THIS BOOK ITSELF IS PROTECTED BY COPYRIGHT LAW. IF YOU REPRODUCED THE WORDS AND IMAGES IN THIS BOOK, IN AN UNAUTHORIZED WAY, I COULD USE THE GUNS OF GOVERNMENT TO STOP YOU.

I'M AGAINST ALL THAT STUFF. BUT IF I DIDN'T COPYRIGHT THIS BOOK IN SOME WAY, YOU COULD CLAIM COPYRIGHT AND STOP ME FROM DISTRIBUTING AND PROFITING FROM MY OWN WORK. INSANE, I KNOW.

AND THE SAME APPLIES TO PATENTS. OVERALL, I DON'T BELIEVE IN INTELLECTUAL PROPERTY. IT'S ANOTHER GOVERNMENT GHOST WITH A GUN.

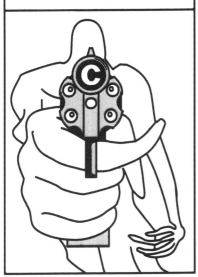

INTELLECTUAL PROPERTY IS THE KIND OF THING THAT IS ONLY PROPERTY IF YOU KEEP IT SECRET AND SUBJECTIVE--OR USE THE GUNS OF GOVERNMENT TO MAKE IT SEEM LIKE PROPERTY.

MR. VOLUNTARY SAYS:

IF YOU CAN'T TOUCH IT WITH YOUR HANDS, IT'S NOT PROPERTY.

ONCE INTELLECTUAL PROPERTY LEAVES THE MIND, IT IS SIMPLY INFORMATION.

INFORMATION, BY ITS VERY NATURE, IS NOT PROPERTY; IT IS INSTEAD A MEDIUM OF EXCHANGE, LIKE LIGHT, SOUND, LANGUAGE, OR EVEN PAPER CURRENCY. INFORMATION CAN BE REPRODUCED INFINITELY. TECHNICALLY, INFORMATION REQUIRES A LITTLE BIT OF ENERGY TO BE REPRODUCED AND STORED. BUT FOR ALL PRACTICAL PURPOSES, IT CAN BE REPRODUCED INFINITELY FOR FREE.

THE EXPRESSION OF INFORMATION IS THE ONLY THING UNIQUE ABOUT IT. AND IF YOU CAN CONTROL THE SCARCITY OF A UNIQUE EXPRESSION THAT PEOPLE WANT, YOU HAVE A PRODUCT.

FOR INSTANCE, IF YOU ARE A MUSICIAN, YOU CAN TRY TO SELL YOUR RECORDED MUSIC, BUT WITHOUT GOVERNMENT GUNS, YOU AREN'T GOING TO STOP PEOPLE FROM SPREADING IT FOR FREE.

NEVER MIND INTELLECTUAL PROPERTY

HERE'S

VOLUNTARYISM

HOWEVER, YOU DO HAVE A UNIQUE EXPRESSION OF YOUR MUSIC TO SELL: LIVE PERFORMANCES. NO ONE CAN PLAY A SONG QUITE LIKE THE PERSON WHO ORIGINALLY WROTE IT, RECORDED IT, AND MADE IT FAMOUS. AND WATCHING A RECORDING OF A LIVE SHOW ISN'T THE SAME AS THE ACTUAL SHOW.

THE **Voluntary experience**

THAT'S A PRODUCT, BUT AN MP3 IS NOT. AN MP3 IS AN ADVERTISEMENT, OR AN APPEAL TO CHARITY.

DOWNLOAD OUR NEWEST SONG HERE

Download

WE SIMPLY ASK THAT YOU DONATE $1 PER DOWNLOAD SO WE CAN AFFORD TO KEEP RECORDING MUSIC FOR YOU.

HOWEVER, A WEBSITE THAT MAKES DOWNLOADING MP3S CONVENIENT, AND ASSURES THAT THE ARTIST OF AN MP3 GETS A GOOD CUT FROM PAID DOWNLOADS, IS A POTENTIAL PRODUCT.

IN GENERAL, IF GOVERNMENT GUNS NEED TO GET INVOLVED TO MAKE SOMETHING A PRODUCT, IT IS NOT A PRODUCT. THE SCARCITY OF REAL PRODUCTS CAN BE CONTROLLED WITHOUT FORCE.

PHYSICAL COPIES OF THIS BOOK ARE A PRODUCT. AND IF YOU OWN A PHYSICAL BOOK, IT IS YOURS.

DIGITAL COPIES OF THIS BOOK ARE NOT REALLY A PRODUCT THOUGH. HOWEVER, MAKING THIS BOOK CONVENIENTLY DOWNLOADABLE IS A PRODUCT.

I TRUST THAT IF YOU VALUE THE EFFORTS I PUT INTO THIS BOOK, YOU'LL VOLUNTARILY COMPENSATE ME IN SOME WAY. BUT I'M NOT GOING TO FORCE YOU TO COMPENSATE ME. THE SCARCITY OF THIS INFORMATION IS MY RESPONSIBILITY, NOT YOURS. TO WAVE A GOVERNMENT GUN IN YOUR FACE FOR SUCH AN ABSTRACT OFFENSE AS INTELLECTUAL PROPERTY INFRINGEMENT WOULD MAKE ME THE AGGRESSOR NOT YOU.

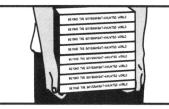

BUT UNFORTUNATELY, THE WORLD IS FILLED WITH INSANE, AGGRESSIVE PEOPLE WHO DON'T SHARE MY SENTIMENT ON SUCH MATTERS.

THE KNEE-JERK REACTION OF THE COMMON SLAVE TO CHALLENGING THE CONCEPT OF INTELLECTUAL PROPERTY IS USUALLY SOMETHING LIKE:

WITHOUT INTELLECTUAL PROPERTY, THERE WOULD BE CHAOS AND PEOPLE COULDN'T MAKE ANY MONEY OFF IDEAS.

THE SIMPLE ANSWER TO THAT IS...BULLSHIT. THERE IS NO INTELLECTUAL PROPERTY IN FASHION. THEY CANNOT PROTECT THEIR DESIGNS. THE ONLY THING THEY CAN DO IS MAKE A SPECIAL TAG OR LOGO STATING THE BRAND. THEREFORE, WHEN YOU BUY CLOTHES, YOU ARE PAYING FOR THE PHYSICAL QUALITY, BRAND NAME, AND CURRENT NOVELTY OF THE ITEM, NOT THE IDEA.

AS MORE AND MORE CLOTHING PRODUCERS COPY A FASHION IDEA, THE IDEA HEADS EVER CLOSER TO ITS TRUE VALUE: ZERO.

THAT'S A GOOD THING, BECAUSE A MARKET IS SUPPOSED TO BRING PRICES DOWN TO AS CLOSE TO ZERO AS POSSIBLE BY MAKING THINGS UBIQUITOUS. INTELLECTUAL PROPERTY LAWS SCREW THAT MECHANISM UP.

INFORMATION'S VALUE DEPENDS ON ITS APPEAL AND NOVELTY. ONCE IT BEGINS TO SPREAD AND REPLICATE, IT LOSES MONETARY VALUE. THAT'S ITS NATURE.

SO, IF YOU DON'T WANT YOUR IDEAS SPREAD, KEEP THEM TO YOURSELF. SEE HOW MUCH MONEY YOU MAKE OFF YOUR IDEAS THAT WAY.

MR. VOLUNTARY SAYS:

IF YOU ARE THE FIRST PERSON WITH AN IDEA, MAKE THAT CLEAR, THEN YOU WILL AT LEAST ALWAYS HAVE THE TOOL OF SOCIAL PRESSURE TO DETER PEOPLE WHO WANT TO TAKE CREDIT FOR YOUR WORK.

THE WRIGHT BROTHERS WERE A PRIME EXAMPLE OF THE COUNTERPRODUCTIVE AND VIOLENT NATURE OF INTELLECTUAL PROPERTY.

THE WRIGHT BROTHERS DIDN'T REALLY INVENT FLIGHT. THEY HAD A LOT OF COMPETITION. BUT THE WRIGHT BROTHERS GOT THE RIGHT PATENT (ON FLIGHT CONTROL) AND SUED LIKE CRAZY.

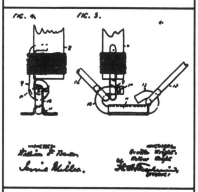

IT WAS SIR GEORGE CAYLEY IN BRITAIN AND OTTO LILIENTHAL OF GERMANY WHO DID THE BULK OF THE WORK OF INVENTING THE AIRPLANE.

DUE TO THE WRIGHT BROTHERS, EARLY UNITED STATES INNOVATION IN AVIATION WAS HINDERED. MOST EARLY INNOVATION ENDED UP TAKING PLACE IN FRANCE.[5]

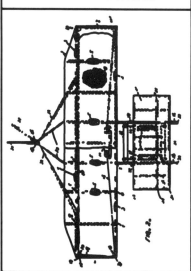

THE COURT SYSTEM IS OF COURSE HOW THE GUNS OF GOVERNMENT INITIATE THE FORCE OF INTELLECTUAL PROPERTY.

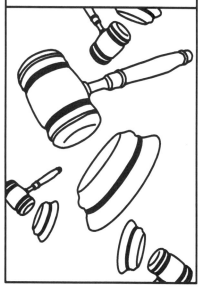

107

AND NEEDLESS TO SAY, A COMPLEX LEGAL SYSTEM KEEPS LAWYERS IN BUSINESS, WHICH IS A FORM OF CORPORATISM.

INFORMATION IS MOST VALUABLE WHEN IT CAN BE FREELY USED TO REMIX AND BUILD UPON. AND IF CONSUMERS SIMPLY STARTED TO BOYCOTT PATENTED AND COPYRIGHTED PRODUCTS, THEN INTELLECTUAL PROPERTY LAWS WOULD BE ABANDONED FOR THE SAKE OF KEEPING CONSUMERS HAPPY. REMEMBER, NO CUSTOMERS NO BUSINESS, WHICH MEANS CONSUMERS HAVE THE POWER TO TAKE THE GUNS OF GOVERNMENT AWAY FROM BUSINESSES.

BREAK THE CHAINS! BUY ONLY PATENT AND COPYRIGHT-FREE PRODUCTS.

IF THERE HAS EVER BEEN AN EXPERIMENT SHOWING HOW INNOVATION IS FOSTERED WHEN IDEAS ARE FREELY DISPERSED, IT IS THE INTERNET.

http://w

THE IDEAS THAT EVENTUALLY LED ME TO WRITE AND DRAW THIS BOOK CAME TO ME FREELY THROUGH THE INTERNET. THE INTERNET ALSO HELPED ME FIND THE RIGHT BOOKS TO BUY FOR RESEARCH.

PEOPLE CAN ENSLAVE BODIES, BUT IDEAS ARE FREE, INCAPABLE OF BEING KEPT IN PRISON OR LIMITED IN ANY WAY EXCEPT BY THE MIND THAT THOUGHT THEM.

AN IDEA REMAINS JOINED TO ITS SOURCE, WHICH IS ITS JAILER OR ITS LIBERATOR, ACCORDING TO WHAT IT CHOOSES AS ITS PURPOSE: AGGRESSION OR PEACE.

WHETHER IT BE PATENTS, INCORPORATION, PRICE FIXING, GOVERNMENT CURRENCY, WHATEVER, IF IT NEEDS A GUN TO EXIST, IT IS MORALLY INDEFENSIBLE.

BECAUSE TO DEFEND ANYTHING THAT REQUIRES A GUN MEANS THAT YOU ULTIMATELY SUPPORT THE USE OF VIOLENCE AGAINST NON-AGGRESSORS.

TAKE YOUR STINKING PAWS OFF ME, YOU DAMN DIRTY STATE!

CHAPTER FIVE

A DAY IN A FREE WORLD

NOW HERE'S THE FUN PART. I'VE GIVEN YOU A GENERAL OVERVIEW SHOWING YOU WHAT A VIOLENT LIE THE GOVERNMENT-HAUNTED WORLD IS. NOW IT IS TIME TO SHOW YOU THE WORLD WITHOUT GOVERNMENT.

GOVERNMENT HAS BEEN TRIED TO DEATH, LITERALLY. BUT NO-GOVERNMENT HASN'T REALLY BEEN TRIED EXCEPT BY ACCIDENT. THEREFORE, I CAN'T POINT TO ANY CLEAR EXAMPLE OF A SOCIETY BUILT COMPLETELY AROUND THE SIMPLE LOGIC OF VOLUNTARYISM.

WHAT I CAN DO THOUGH IS EXTRAPOLATE THE VOLUNTARYISM THAT ALREADY EXISTS WITHIN GOVERNMENT SOCIETIES TO SHOW WHAT TOTAL VOLUNTARYISM MIGHT BE LIKE.

IN OTHER WORDS, I CAN SHOW YOU WHAT A WORLD OF RULES WITHOUT RULERS MIGHT BE LIKE: THE KIND OF WORLD THAT WOULD BE EXPECTED BY ANY INTELLIGENT BEING.

DO YOU WANT ME TO TAKE YOU TO OUR LEADER?

WHAT'S A LEADER?

I CAN'T TELL YOU EXACTLY WHAT A TOTALLY VOLUNTARY SOCIETY WOULD BE LIKE SINCE ONE OF THE MAIN POINTS OF VOLUNTARYISM IS THAT IT ALLOWS PEOPLE TO CONSTANTLY, FREELY TEST IDEAS TO FIND OUT WHAT WORKS BEST...INSTEAD OF RELYING ON THE CLUELESS DIRECTIVES OF A DELUSIONAL CENTRALIZED AUTHORITY.

WHAT I CAN GUARANTEE THOUGH IS THAT IT WILL BE A MUCH MORE EFFICIENT, PROSPEROUS, AND PEACEFUL SOCIETY. THAT'S BECAUSE A VOLUNTARYIST SOCIETY HAS ALL THE FEEDBACK MECHANISMS TO FACILITATE EFFICIENCY, PROSPERITY, AND PEACE.

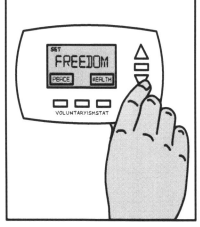

IF GOVERNMENT REALLY CARED ABOUT FIGURING OUT WHAT WOULD WORK BEST TO ORGANIZE SOCIETY, GOVERNMENT WOULD HAVE PURPOSELY RELINQUISHED ITS POWER TO CERTAIN REGIONS FOR THE SAKE OF EXPERIMENTATION A LONG TIME AGO.

BUT THE REALITY IS THAT IF GOVERNMENT EVER ALLOWED THE EXPERIMENT OF A VOLUNTARY SOCIETY TO ARISE, GOVERNMENT WOULD USHER IN ITS OWN DEMISE. THE EVIDENCE WOULD BECOME CLEAR.

ALL INNOVATIVE MINDS HEAD TO VOLUNTARY LAND AND PROSPER!

BUT ANYWAY, BACK TO OUR HYPOTHETICAL DAY IN A FREE WORLD. FOR THE SAKE OF SIMPLICITY, THE FREE WORLD WE ARE GOING TO TOUR IS THE SAME CONTEMPORARY WORLD WE ALREADY KNOW, EXCEPT WITHOUT GOVERNMENT.

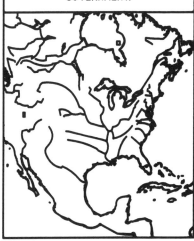

ALL I'M GOING TO DO IS ASSUME A FEW THINGS TECHNOLOGICALLY THAT WE COULD POSSIBLY EXPECT FROM A VOLUNTARYIST SOCIETY COMPARED TO THE PRESENT REPRESSED GOVERNMENT SOCIETY.

I START THE DAY WAKING UP. I LIVE IN A SOMEWHAT NORMAL HOUSE AND SLEEP IN A NORMAL BED.

FIRST THING I DO IS TAKE A LEAK OF COURSE, BUT THEN I TURN ON THE COMPUTER AND CHECK UP ON EMAILS.

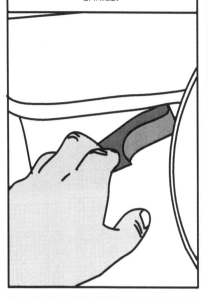

EARNING MONEY FOR THE DAY DOESN'T EVEN REQUIRE ME LEAVING THE HOUSE. I WRITE AND ILLUSTRATE COMIC BOOKS, I SELL PAINTINGS, AND I DESIGN OBJECTS FOR CLIENTS THAT ARE PRODUCED USING MICRO MANUFACTURING CONSISTING MOSTLY OF 3D PRINTERS. JUST A FEW HOURS OF WORK A DAY KEEPS MY CURRENCY ACCOUNT FULL OF ALL THE MONEY I NEED TO LIVE COMFORTABLY AND THEN SOME.

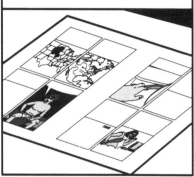

I DON'T HAVE TO KEEP ANY PAPERWORK BECAUSE I DON'T HAVE TO PAY ANY TAXES. THE COST OF DOING BUSINESS CONSISTS MERELY OF A COMPUTER, A SUPER HIGH-SPEED INTERNET CONNECTION, AND OCCASIONALLY I NEED TO PAY TO HAVE A CONTRACT WITH A CLIENT ASSURED. IN FACT, I NEED TO CHECK ON GETTING A CLIENT CONTRACT ASSURED TODAY.

SUPER EZ 1040

JUST SIGN, BURN, AND NEVER WORRY ABOUT PAYING TAXES EVER AGAIN

U.S. Individual Income Tax Return

Label					OMB No. 1545-0074
See instructions on page 12.	L A B E L	Your first name and initial		Last name	Your social security number
Use the IRS label. Otherwise, please print or type.	H E R E	If a joint return, spouse's first name and initial		Last name	Spouse's social security number
		Home address (number and street). If you have a P.O. box, see page 12.		Apt. no.	You must enter your SSN(s) above.
		City, town or post office, state, and ZIP code. If you have a foreign address, see page 12.			Checking a box below will not change your tax or refund.
Presidential Election Campaign ▶					☐ You ☐ Spouse
Filing Status Check only one box.	1 ☐ Single			4 ☐ Head of household (with qualifying person). (See page 1	
	2 ☐ Married filing jointly (even if only one had income)			the qualifying person is a child but not your dependent, e	
	3 ☐ Married filing separately. Enter spouse's SSN above and full name here. ▶			the child's name here. ▶	
				5 ☐ Qualifying widow(er) with dependent child (see page	

ASSURANCE IS SIMILAR TO WHAT WAS CALLED INSURANCE IN GOVERNMENT SOCIETY. BUT SINCE INSURANCE WAS ALL TOO OFTEN JUST A CORRUPT, QUASI-GOVERNMENTAL SCAM BACK IN THE GOVERNMENT WORLD, THE WORD ASSURANCE TOOK ITS PLACE AS VOLUNTARYISM AROSE.

SUCH A SCAM ONLY A CAVEMAN WOULD BUY IT.

INSURANCE BACK IN THE GOVERNMENT WORLD WAS JUST CORPORATIST SOCIALISM. IN OTHER WORDS, IT WAS A BIG SCAM.

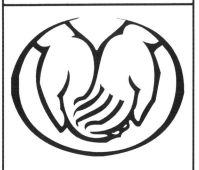

ARE YOU IN CORPORATIST HANDS?

IN VOLUNTARY SOCIETY, INSURANCE IS ASSURANCE AND IT ACTS AS VOLUNTARY SOCIALISM AND ALSO VOLUNTARY SECURITY. ASSURANCE ACTS AS THE ENTITY THAT ALLOWS FOR RULES WITHOUT RULERS. ASSURANCE IS A FREE MARKET OF RULES WITHOUT GOVERNMENT.

MR. VOLUNTARY SAYS:

ALL GOVERNMENTS RELY ON COERCIVE SOCIALISM TO SOME DEGREE.

THIS CLIENT OF MINE WANTS ME TO PRODUCE A BUNCH OF PRINTABLE FILES FOR SOME UNIQUE, COMPLEX, ORNATE MOULDING FEATURES FOR HIS HIGH-END HOME REMODELING BUSINESS. I'M ABLE TO LOOK THIS GUY UP ON THE WEBSITE OF THE ASSURER I USE. AND I CAN TELL THAT THE ONLY TARNISH ON HIS REPUTATION IS THAT HE RAN OUT OF MONEY AT LEAST ONCE.

I HAVE A SPOTLESS REPUTATION, SO ASSURANCE FOR ME IS VERY CHEAP. MY SPOTLESS RECORD MEANS I CAN GET PEOPLE TO PAY ME ONE HUNDRED PERCENT UP FRONT. SO, THAT IS WHAT I'M GOING TO TRY TO DO WITH THIS GUY. IF HE CAN'T, I'LL CHARGE HIM A LITTLE MORE AND GET HIS PROMISE TO PAY ASSURED. THAT WAY HE'LL BE EVEN MORE OBLIGATED NOT TO STIFF ME.

I DON'T LIKE EATING NORMAL BREAKFAST FOODS FOR BREAKFAST, SO I USUALLY HAVE SOMETHING LIKE A TURKEY SANDWICH. WHILE I EAT, I TURN ON THE NEWS TO SEE WHAT IS UP.

THERE IS STILL NEWS BUT THE NEWS IS ACTUALLY CONCERNED WITH THE TRUTH NOT JUST PROPAGANDA. THERE ARE NO POLITICS TO COVER AFTER ALL. AND THERE ISN'T OFTEN MUCH CRIME TO COVER ON THE NEWS. WHEN THERE IS A CRIME COMMITTED AND THE EVIDENCE OF THE CRIME IS CLEAR, THE NEWS DEVASTATES THE REPUTATION OF THE CRIMINALS. CRIME TRULY DOESN'T PAY IN A FREE SOCIETY.

WE ALL BUY GENERAL ASSURANCE TO PROTECT OTHERS FROM OUR OWN POTENTIAL NEGLIGENCE. IF YOU DON'T HAVE SOME KIND OF GENERAL ASSURANCE, IT IS ACCEPTED PRACTICE TO EXCLUDE YOU FROM BUSINESS TRANSACTIONS--WHICH MEANS YOU CAN'T EVEN BUY A LOAF OF BREAD, BECAUSE YOU PROBABLY DON'T HAVE A CURRENCY ACCOUNT.

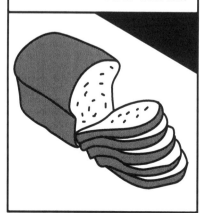

PLUS, IT IS JUST NOT WORTH ASSISTING SOMEONE WHO DOESN'T ABIDE BY THE SIMPLE RULES OF THE VOLUNTARYIST SOCIETY.

COMMANDMENTS

I. NON-AGGRESSION: DO UNTO OTHERS AS YOU WOULD HAVE THEM DO UNTO YOU.

II. PRIVATE PROPERTY: DO NOT STEAL OR HARM PHYSICAL PROPERTY THAT ISN'T YOUR OWN.

III. BE HONEST AND BE COOL.

GENERAL ASSURANCE IS THE FUNDAMENTAL FEEDBACK MECHANISM THAT KEEPS EVERYONE LIVING A LIFE FREE OF THE INITIATION OF FORCE.

LOSE MONEY

INITIATE FORCE

KEEP AND MAKE MONEY

INTERACT VOLUNTARILY

IN A WAY, ASSURERS ARE LIKE A FREE MARKET OF GOVERNMENTS. WITH ASSURERS COME RULE SYSTEMS WITHOUT RULERS. THE ASSURERS ARE ONLY REQUIRED TO AGREE TO THE NON-AGGRESSION PRINCIPLE AND THE BASICS OF PHYSICAL PROPERTY RIGHTS.

IF YOU DAMAGE OTHER PEOPLE'S PROPERTY, STEAL, INITIATE FORCE, OR DO ANYTHING ELSE THAT'S UNACCEPTABLE UNDER THE PRECEPTS OF VOLUNTARYISM, THEN YOUR ASSURER IS OBLIGATED TO SETTLE ON SOME REASONABLE FORM OF COMPENSATION.

BUT IF YOU ARE GOING TO ACCUSE SOMEONE OF SOMETHING, YOU DAMN WELL BETTER HAVE SOME GOOD EVIDENCE, BECAUSE FALSE CLAIMS ARE THEMSELVES DEEMED AN INITIATION OF FORCE. AND SO, YOU CAN FIND YOURSELF PAYING MUCH HIGHER ASSURANCE OR OUTRIGHT DROPPED IF YOU ACCUSE BUT HAVE INADEQUATE OR FALSIFIED EVIDENCE.

THE SAME APPLIES IF YOU GO AROUND TRYING TO SPREAD LIES ABOUT PEOPLE IN GENERAL. WHAT YOU SAY BETTER BE TRUE.

THERE ARE CHARITABLE GENERAL ASSURERS FOR PEOPLE WHO CAN'T AFFORD IT. BUT GENERAL ASSURANCE IS BIG BUSINESS AND THEREFORE IT'S SO COMPETITIVE AND CHEAP THAT YOU REALLY HAVE TO BE A BUM NOT TO BE ABLE TO AFFORD IT.

CRIME NEVER PAYS IN VOLUNTARYIST SOCIETY. WHICH IS TO SAY, THE INITIATION OF FORCE NEVER PAYS. BEING LOCKED UP IN A CAGE THAT IS FUNDED BY COERCION IS A WALK IN THE PARK COMPARED TO THE PROSPECT OF BEING OSTRACIZED.

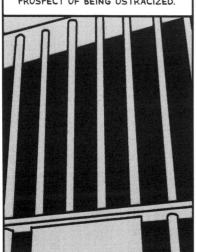

YOU CAN'T EVEN APPEAL TO FRIENDS AND FAMILY TO BAIL YOU OUT IF YOU CAN'T GET GENERAL ASSURANCE, BECAUSE AIDING A CRIMINAL IS A SURE WAY TO GET GENERAL ASSURANCE PROBLEMS.

THE MORE OPEN YOU ARE TO PROVE THAT YOU ARE PLAYING BY THE RULES, THE CHEAPER IT IS TO ASSURE EVERYTHING.

PEOPLE WHO SCREW UP AND BECOME OSTRACIZED EITHER DO WHAT THEY NEED TO DO TO RESTORE A GOOD STANDING, OR THEY COMMIT SUICIDE. THAT'S THE REALITY. ONLY A FEW PEOPLE EVER SUCCESSFULLY DISAPPEAR INTO THE WILDERNESS TO LIVE OFF THE LAND.

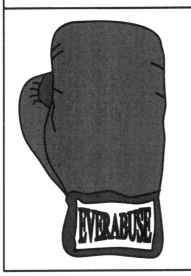

IF YOU ABUSE YOUR KIDS OR ABUSE YOUR SPOUSE, THAT KIND OF STUFF TOO TRANSLATES INTO GENERAL ASSURANCE PROBLEMS...AND THE POSSIBILITY OF BEING OSTRACIZED.

EVERABUSE

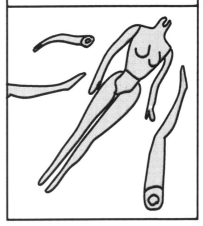

ABUSED CHILDREN DISPLAY BEHAVIORAL TRAITS THAT PUT UP A BIG RED FLAG FOR ASSURERS. SO, ALTHOUGH YOU MAY BE ABLE TO GET AWAY WITH AGGRESSIVE, UNACCEPTABLE BEHAVIOR FOR AWHILE BEHIND CLOSED DOORS, IT WILL EVENTUALLY COME TO THE SURFACE AND COST YOU.

IN A VOLUNTARYIST SOCIETY, YOU ARE INDEED THE MASTER OF YOUR OWN DESTINY. FOLLOW THE SIMPLE, LOGICAL RULES OF VOLUNTARYIST SOCIETY AND THE COST OF SECURITY IS TINY.

THE FREE MARKET ASSURANCE SYSTEM OF OUR VOLUNTARYIST SOCIETY TRULY MAKES GOVERNMENT LOOK COMPLETELY BARBARIC. TO THINK THAT PEOPLE USED TO ENSLAVE THEMSELVES TO GOVERNMENTS JUST TO GET MANY OF THE SERVICES ASSURERS NOW PROVIDE IS MIND BLOWING.

AS I ALREADY MENTIONED, BUSINESS CONTRACTS ARE ASSURED WHENEVER DEEMED NECESSARY. THAT CREATES A DATABASE OF BUSINESS REPUTATIONS. AND IT REQUIRES NO GUNS TO FORCE PEOPLE TO CONDUCT HONEST BUSINESS. IT'S ALL ABOUT MONEY AND REPUTATION.

TECHNICALLY, GENERAL ASSURANCE COVERS BOTCHED BUSINESS CONTRACTS AND INTERACTIONS, BUT UNLESS YOU GET A CONTRACT SPECIFICALLY ASSURED, YOU CAN YOURSELF BE PENALIZED BY HIGHER ASSURANCE COSTS IF A CONTRACT OR TRANSACTION REQUIRES AN ASSURANCE PAYOUT.

119

SPECIFIC ASSURANCE KEEPS GENERAL ASSURANCE AS CHEAP AS IT IS. SPECIFIC ASSURANCE MAKES PEOPLE TAKE MORE PERSONAL RESPONSIBILITY FOR THEIR SPECIFIC INTERACTIONS, BECAUSE GENERAL ASSURANCE IS MOSTLY ABOUT PROTECTING OTHER PEOPLE FROM YOU, NOT PROTECTING YOU YOURSELF.

HEALTH ASSURANCE IS A FORM OF SPECIFIC ASSURANCE.

HEALTH ASSURANCE IS VERY CHEAP, ESPECIALLY IF YOU ARE WILLING TO PROVE HOW HEALTHY YOU ARE. THE HEALTH SYSTEM IS OBVIOUSLY COMPLETELY FREE MARKET, SO THERE IS A LOT OF COMPETITION AND THERE ARE A LOT OF OPTIONS. DOCTORS ACTUALLY ADVERTISE PRICES, INSTEAD OF SURPRISING YOU WITH A BILL LATER.

THERE WERE SOME ASSURERS THAT TRIED TO RUN THEIR OWN HEALTHCARE SYSTEMS EXCLUSIVELY FOR THEIR OWN CLIENTS, BUT THE COST-TO-QUALITY BALANCE FAILED TO KEEP THEM COMPETITIVE.

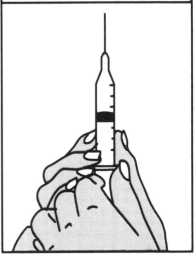

MOST ASSURANCE ONLY COVERS MAJOR HEALTH EVENTS, NOT COMMON STUFF. THAT KEEPS PRICES LOW SINCE PEOPLE ARE PAYING FOR HEALTH SERVICES OUT OF POCKET.

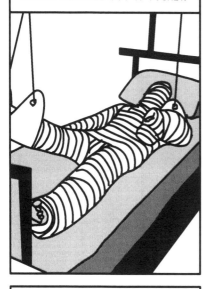

PHARMACEUTICALS ARE FOR THE MOST PART VERY CHEAP SINCE THERE ARE NO GUNS PROTECTING MONOPOLIES ON DRUG FORMULAS. KEEPING SECRETS IS UP TO THE SECRET HOLDERS.

THEREFORE, IN THE CASE OF VERY NICHE SMALL MARKET DRUGS, IN ORDER TO KEEP THAT KIND OF PHARMACEUTICAL RESEARCH AND DEVELOPMENT ECONOMICAL, ASSURED CONFIDENTIALITY AGREEMENTS BETWEEN DRUG COMPANIES AND USERS ARE SOMETIMES REQUIRED. BUT THAT KIND OF THING IS VERY RARE.

ASSURERS HAVE A CLEAR INCENTIVE TO PREVENT THE THINGS THAT WOULD LEAD TO THEM PAYING OUT. THEREFORE, ASSURERS FUND THINGS LIKE SECURITY MEASURES. OFTEN THOSE MEASURES ARE OF A TECHNOLOGICAL NATURE, LIKE SURVEILLANCE. BUT THOSE MEASURES ALSO INCLUDE ACTUAL SECURITY PERSONNEL.

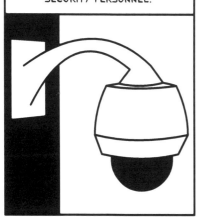

ASSURERS ALSO FUND ALL KINDS OF EDUCATION. AND TAKING SPECIFIC CLASSES CAN LOWER ASSURANCE COSTS. FOR EXAMPLE, THERE ARE CLASSES ON HOW TO RAISE GOOD, PEACEFUL, EMPATHETIC CHILDREN. THERE ARE CLASSES ON HOW TO MAKE SAFE BUSINESS DEALS. THERE ARE SELF-DEFENSE CLASSES. THERE ARE HEALTH CLASSES.

AND ASSURERS GUIDE THE EDUCATION OF CHILDREN TOO. CHILDREN ARE ASSURED AS PART OF THEIR PARENTS' GENERAL ASSURANCE UNTIL THEY ARE 14 ON MOST POLICIES.

CHILDREN ARE FREE TO BE EDUCATED ANY WAY THE PARENTS WANT. THERE ARE STILL SCHOOLS IN THE TRADITIONAL SENSE OF PLACES CHILDREN GO TO LEARN, BUT SUCH SCHOOLS ARE REALLY JUST DAYCARE COMBINED WITH SCHOOLING FOR CHILDREN WHOSE PARENTS CAN'T STAY HOME WITH THEIR CHILDREN EVERY DAY.

DING
DING
DING

WE HAVE REACHED THE ARBITRARY TIME UPON WHICH WE MUST STOP THINKING ABOUT OUR STATE APPROVED VIEW OF HISTORY AND INSTEAD TURN OUR ATTENTION TO MATH.

SINCE I'M NOT GOING TO MAKE YOU SIT AND WATCH ME WORK AT THE COMPUTER ALL DAY. LET'S TAKE A TRIP TO MY SISTER'S HOUSE AND I'LL SHOW YOU WHAT EDUCATION IS LIKE FOR MY FIVE-YEAR-OLD NEPHEW. JUST LET ME GET A FEW THINGS AND WE'LL GO.

I LOCK UP MY HOUSE BEFORE LEAVING, BUT THE REALITY IS THAT I COULD PROBABLY LEAVE THE DOORS WIDE OPEN FOR 20 YEARS BEFORE ANYONE EVER TRIED TO STEAL ANYTHING.

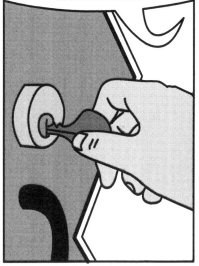

TAKE A LOOK AT MY HOUSE FROM THE OUTSIDE. THERE IS A LOT OF SUBTLE OUTSIDE SURVEILLANCE IN CASE I EVER NEED TO BUILD A CASE AGAINST SOMEONE LIKE A THIEF OR VANDAL.

INSIDE I HAVE A FEW NON-LETHAL WEAPONS IF NEEDED. IN OUR COMMUNITY, THE ONLY PEOPLE THAT USE GUNS FOR DEFENSE ARE PEOPLE WHO WANT TO KILL PEOPLE. SUCH PEOPLE ARE ASSURANCE RISKS.

AT THE PEAK OF THE HOUSE AND BELOW THE HOUSE ARE POLLUTION MONITORS; THEY WORK IN TANDEM WITH OTHER MONITORS ON OTHER PROPERTIES AND KEEP TRACK OF ANY EXCESS POLLUTION SOMEONE MIGHT BE PRODUCING.

IF I CRANKED UP A FEW BIG GASOLINE ENGINES, OR CRANKED UP AN OLD STEREO (STEREOS MADE IN VOLUNTARY SOCIETY ARE ALL DESIGNED TO CONTAIN SOUND), THEN THAT TOP MONITOR WOULD LIKELY START PRODUCING A WARNING.

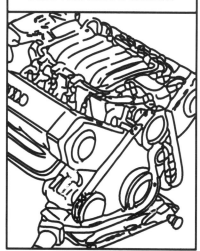

IF I FAILED TO STOP POLLUTING WITHIN 30 MINUTES, OR STARTED POLLUTING AGAIN WITHIN 48 HOURS, MY POLLUTION WOULD BECOME PUBLIC KNOWLEDGE IN THE POLLUTION DATABASE AND ANYONE WHO CARED TO BUILD A CASE AGAINST ME, SUCH AS NEIGHBORS, WOULD BE ABLE TO FILE A LEGITIMATE POLLUTION CLAIM.

SO, NEEDLESS TO SAY, WE LIVE CLEAN, RESPECTFUL LIVES IN THIS NEIGHBORHOOD. DIFFERENT COMMUNITIES HAVE SLIGHTLY DIFFERENT POLLUTION STANDARDS, BUT ALL ASSURED PEOPLE ARE OBLIGATED TO FOLLOWING STANDARDS.

MOST HOMES HAVE SOME KIND OF AUTONOMOUS POWER SYSTEM INSTALLED THAT FEEDS INTO A POWER GRID. ON MINE, I HAVE A FUEL CELL SYSTEM.

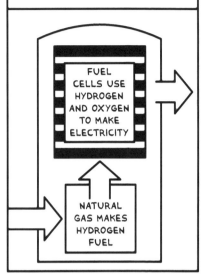

FUEL CELLS USE HYDROGEN AND OXYGEN TO MAKE ELECTRICITY

NATURAL GAS MAKES HYDROGEN FUEL

MY FUEL CELL SYSTEM HELPS CHARGE MY CAR, WHICH IS A REBUILT 1981 DELOREAN THAT RUNS PRIMARILY ON ELECTRICITY, BUT ALSO HAS A SMALL FUEL CELL SYSTEM. GASOLINE CARS ARE EXPENSIVE, DUE TO THE COST OF POLLUTION CONTAINMENT AND CONTROL. THEY ARE NOW MERELY NOVELTIES.

THE ROADS IN MY COMMUNITY ARE A RELIC OF THE OLD GOVERNMENT. THE FUNDING OF ROADS BY GOVERNMENT GAVE AUTOMOBILES A NEAR MONOPOLY ON TRANSPORTATION. AND AUTOMOBILE POLLUTION WAS THUS FACILITATED BY GOVERNMENT.

WITHOUT GOVERNMENT, ROADS LIKE THESE WOULDN'T EXIST, WE'D LIKELY HAVE SOMETHING ELSE. UPON THE DISSOLUTION OF THE GOVERNMENT, WHOEVER OWNED THE PROPERTY ADJACENT TO A ROAD BECAME OWNER OF THAT SECTION OF ROAD. AND BY ACCEPTING OWNERSHIP, THE PERSON BECAME CONTRACTUALLY OBLIGATED TO KEEP THE ROAD OPEN AND MAINTAINED AS PART OF THE LARGER ROAD SYSTEM.

MANY PEOPLE THEN SOLD OFF THEIR PIECES TO INVESTORS FOR QUICK CASH, BUT I PERSONALLY OWN ONE HUNDRED FEET OF THIS HALF OF THE ROAD SINCE IT WAS INCLUDED WITH THE PURCHASE OF THIS PROPERTY.

A GENERAL ROAD COMPANY TAKES CARE OF THE ROAD MAINTENANCE AND TOLL COLLECTION FOR EVERYONE, BUT I ACTUALLY MAKE A LITTLE TOLL MONEY OFF THIS SECTION OF ROAD. THE TOLL MONEY I MAKE GOES RIGHT INTO MY TOLL ACCOUNT TO FUND MY OWN DRIVING.

THIS ROAD IS OPERATED BY **TOLL UNITED**

ROADS THAT GET LESS TRAFFIC, LIKE RURAL AND RESIDENTIAL ROADS, TEND TO HAVE HIGHER TOLLS.

DUE TO THE PROFIT MOTIVE, CONTRACTUAL OBLIGATION, AND THE EVER-PRESENT PROSPECT OF BEING OSTRACIZED, EVERYONE WHO OWNS A PIECE OF ROAD COMPLIES WITH KEEPING THE SYSTEM OPEN FOR BUSINESS.

NOTE: THE SAME RULES APPLY TO PEOPLE WHO OWN PORTIONS OF OTHER TRANSPORTATION SYSTEMS, SUCH AS RIVERS.

TO RIDE ON ANY OF THE ROADS IN MY COMMUNITY YOU HAVE TO HAVE A SUITABLE CAR. FIRST OFF, THE CAR HAS TO BE POLLUTION SAFE IN TERMS OF BOTH EMISSIONS AND NOISE.

IF YOU TOOK A RIDE DOWN A RESIDENTIAL ROAD ON AN OLD STINKING, NOISY MOTORCYCLE, YOU'D BE SEEN AS JUST A HUGE DOUCHE AND YOU'D BE KICKED OFF THE ROAD. THESE DAYS A COOL MOTORCYCLE IS ONE THAT LOOKS WICKED COOL, IS SUPER ENERGY EFFICIENT, FAST, AND QUIET.

SECOND OFF, THE CAR NEEDS TO HAVE AN ELECTRONIC TOLL PAYING SYSTEM INSTALLED WITH A FUNDED ACCOUNT. THERE ARE NO TOLLBOOTHS; TOLLBOOTHS ARE CONTRACTUALLY NOT PERMITTED.

AND THIRD OFF, YOU HAVE TO BE AN ASSURER APPROVED DRIVER AND HAVE AT LEAST GENERAL ASSURANCE.

IN OUR COMMUNITY, THE PLAN IS TO MOVE TO ALL SELF-DRIVING VEHICLES IN FIVE YEARS. AND IN THE NEW SYSTEM, YOU WON'T EVEN HAVE TO OWN YOUR OWN VEHICLE. YOU'LL BE ABLE TO ORDER ONE TO PICK YOU UP AND TAKE YOU WHEREVER YOU WANT TO GO.

IT WILL BE REALLY COOL. BUT IT MEANS THAT FIVE YEARS FROM NOW, MY AWESOME DELOREAN REBUILD WON'T BE ALLOWED ON THESE ROADS.

SO ANYWAY, LET'S GO TO MY SISTER'S HOUSE.

TOLL
0.04
NEW TRIP

SEE HOW MY TOLL TALLY IS DISPLAYED FOR ME?

SIX MILES AND EIGHTEEN CENTS LATER WE ARE AT OUR DESTINATION.

LET'S GO SEE MY NEPHEW.

TOLL
0.18
RESET

HI, I DIDN'T KNOW YOU WERE COMING OVER.

YEAH, BUT DON'T GET EXCITED, I'M ONLY GOING TO BE HERE FOR A MINUTE. I'LL SEE YOU LATER THOUGH. JUST CONTINUE PLAYING.

AS YOU CAN SEE, HE'S PLAYING VIDEO GAMES. SINCE HE LIKES VIDEO GAMES SO MUCH, MY SISTER ENROLLED HIM IN A SCHOOL THAT TEACHES VIRTUALLY USING VIDEO GAMES. THAT'S THE MOST POPULAR KIND OF SCHOOL FOR MALES.

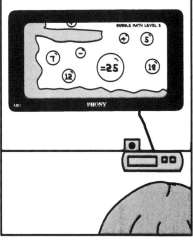

RIGHT NOW, THE CONCENTRATION IS ON LEARNING TO READ, WRITE, AND DO MATH. THERE ARE NO GRADES. HE EITHER LEARNS AND PASSES ON TO THE NEXT LEVEL OR KEEPS PLAYING UNTIL HE DOES.

HE HAS THE OPTION OF PLAYING AGAINST OTHER KIDS. HIS PEER GROUP IS NOT DICTATED BY AGE BUT BY ABILITY LEVEL. HIS FAVORITE COMPETITORS ARE HIS COUSINS, WHO ARE ALSO ENROLLED IN VIDEO GAME SCHOOL. BUT THEY USUALLY AREN'T ON THE SAME LEVELS.

THE CONTROLLERS AND SOUND/VIDEO DETECTORS DETECT WHO'S PLAYING, SO YOU CAN'T CHEAT. AS HE PROGRESSES, HE'LL HAVE MORE FREEDOM IN WHAT HE LEARNS. THAT WAY HE'LL BE ABLE TO MATCH HIS LEARNING WITH HIS CHANGING INTERESTS.

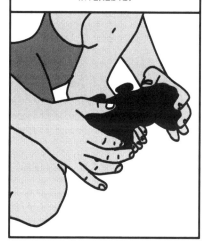

THEN EVENTUALLY, HIS EDUCATION WILL BECOME MORE CAREER ORIENTED. AND IF HE PURSUES THE RIGHT CAREER EDUCATION, IT WILL ACTUALLY BE FREE. BECAUSE MANY INDUSTRIES NEED PEOPLE WITH CERTAIN KNOWLEDGE AND SO ARE WILLING TO FUND FREE EDUCATION.

BUT THE WAY TECHNOLOGY IS PROGRESSING, IN 15 TO 20 YEARS FROM NOW HE MIGHT NOT EVEN NEED TO WORRY ABOUT WORKING.

THE ULTIMATE GOAL OF THE VOLUNTARYIST ECONOMY IS 100% UNEMPLOYMENT. WHICH IS TO SAY THAT THE ULTIMATE GOAL IS TO USE TECHNOLOGY TO DO ALL THE WORK NEEDED IN THE WORLD. THAT WAY THE HUMAN RACE WILL BASICALLY BE ABLE TO RETIRE AND JUST SIT BACK AND RELAX AND DO WHATEVER IT WANTS.

ALL ANYONE WILL NEED TO KNOW TO LIVE AN ABUNDANT LIFE IS A LITTLE BIT ABOUT HOW TO USE AND MAINTAIN TECHNOLOGY. THAT'S HOW EFFICIENT THINGS SHOULD EVENTUALLY GET.

EVEN NOW, THINGS ARE VERY EFFICIENT. WHAT I DO FOR A GOOD LIVING AMOUNTS TO ABOUT THREE HOURS OF WORK A DAY WHEN I ADD IT ALL UP.

SO ANYWAY, THAT'S EDUCATION IN A NUTSHELL: IT'S SIMPLE, EFFICIENT, EFFECTIVE, AND FUN.

NEXT, LET'S GO SEE MY GIRLFRIEND. SHE WAS ALREADY GONE AND AT WORK WHEN I WOKE UP THIS MORNING.

EVEN THOUGH MY GIRLFRIEND IS BASICALLY MY WIFE, THE TERM WIFE IS ONLY USED WHEN TWO PEOPLE HAVE A KID TOGETHER. THERE'S NO PHONY GOVERNMENT MARRIAGE. MARRIAGE IS JUST A PRIVATE CONTRACT.

MY GIRLFRIEND AND I OBVIOUSLY LIVE TOGETHER, BUT THE ONLY CONTRACT WE HAVE WITH EACH OTHER IS AN ACCIDENTAL PREGNANCY CONTRACT. IT KEEPS HER ASSURANCE LOWER.

SO, HERE'S WHERE MY GIRLFRIEND WORKS. THIS IS BASICALLY A BANK.

WHAT PEOPLE USED TO REFER TO AS BANKS ARE NOW BETTER DESCRIBED AS PRIVATE CURRENCY PAYMENT MANAGERS. PENNYWISE IS THE PRIVATE CURRENCY PAYMENT MANAGER I PREDOMINANTLY USE.

WITHOUT GOVERNMENT MONEY, THERE ARE COMPANIES THAT MANAGE PRIVATE CURRENCIES AND PAYMENT SYSTEMS.

PENNYWISE

OKAY, BEHIND THIS DOOR SHOULD BE MY GIRLFRIEND.

KNOCK KNOCK

COME IN.

OH GOODIE, I HOPE YOU CAME BEARING GOOD NEWS.

YEP, THE GOOD NEWS IS THAT YOU LIVE IN AN ALTERNATE UNIVERSE COMPARED TO MY FRIEND HERE WHO LIVES IN A WORLD STILL HAUNTED BY GOVERNMENT.

WELL, THIS SHOULD AT LEAST ACT AS SOME MOTIVATION FOR YOUR FRIEND.

SO EXPLAIN WHAT PENNYWISE DOES.

WE OPERATE WITHIN AN ELABORATE ELECTRONIC SYSTEM THAT MONITORS THE SUPPLY AND USE OF PRIVATE CURRENCIES. THIS SYSTEM ALLOWS EASY CONVERTIBILITY.

AND IT PROVIDES THE FEEDBACK MECHANISMS NEEDED FOR ALL THE PRIVATE CURRENCY PROVIDERS TO MAINTAIN A STABLE VALUE TO THEIR CURRENCY BY KEEPING ITS SUPPLY STABLE.

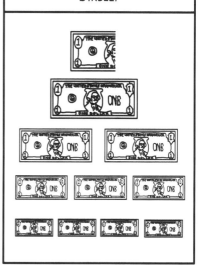

THE MONEY IN THE SYSTEM IS FOR THE MOST PART CREDIT THAT IS ISSUED INTEREST FREE FOR SIX MONTHS. THAT MEANS MOST OF THE MONEY IN THE SYSTEM NEVER REQUIRES INTEREST PAYMENTS. IT'S JUST A BIG BACK AND FORTH WHERE PEOPLE PAY OFF THEIR OLD CREDIT WITH OTHER PEOPLES CREDIT.

THE BETTER YOUR REPUTATION OF CREATING CREDIT WITHOUT NEEDING TO PAY INTEREST, THE MORE ACCESS TO CREDIT YOU HAVE.

133

SINCE THE CURRENCY MANAGEMENT COMPANIES UNDERSTAND MATH, THEY KNOW THAT TOO MANY PEOPLE PAYING TOO MUCH INTEREST MEANS INEVITABLE DEFAULT FOR MANY. THE ONLY OTHER OPTION IS TO ISSUE MORE MONEY TO PAY THE INTEREST, THUS LEADING TO POTENTIAL CURRENCY DEVALUATION.

CURRENCY MANAGEMENT COMPANIES WANT NEITHER OF THOSE THINGS. HERE AT PENNYWISE, WE MAKE OUR PROFITS FROM A WHOLE LOT OF MICROSCOPIC TRANSACTION FEES, NOT INTEREST. INTEREST IS JUST A TOOL FOR MAKING SURE PEOPLE PAY BACK THEIR CURRENCY.

LONGER-TERM, MONEY THAT IS SAVED IS SAVED IN THE FORM OF FINITE PRECIOUS ASSETS LIKE GOLD AND SILVER.

PEOPLE WHO SAVE AND TRANSACT USING PENNYWISE ARE ABLE TO MICRO LEND TO PEOPLE WANTING TO BORROW MONEY USING THE PENNYWISE ONLINE LENDING MARKET.

INTEREST RATES ARE VERY LOW THOUGH, BECAUSE SHORT-TERM RATES FOR MOST PEOPLE ARE ZERO AND SAVINGS IS USUALLY GREATER THAN THE DESIRE TO BORROW. MOST MICRO-LENDING IS THUS JUST TO FRIENDS AND RELATIVES.

A LOT OF SAVED MONEY IS INSTEAD LENT TO BUSINESSES THROUGH THE STOCK MARKET. BUT THE STOCK MARKET ISN'T THE SAME THING AS IN THE GOVERNMENT WORLD. WITHOUT INFLATION, THE STOCK MARKET CAN'T BE EXPECTED TO JUST GO UP INDEFINITELY LONG-TERM. YOU CAN'T JUST THROW MONEY INTO THE STOCK MARKET AND GO WITH THE FLOW, BECAUSE THE OVERALL FLOW IS USUALLY FLAT. YOU HAVE TO INVEST IN COMPANIES THAT HAVE AMAZING POTENTIAL.

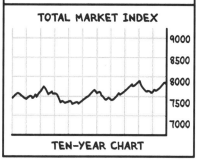

TOTAL MARKET INDEX

9000
8500
8000
7500
7000

TEN-YEAR CHART

THE OVERALL ECONOMIC GOAL IS NOT GROWTH BUT EFFICIENCY. PEOPLE DON'T TALK ABOUT GROWTH ANYMORE, THEY TALK ABOUT EFFICIENCY. THE OLD-FASHIONED OBSESSION WITH GROWTH WAS A RESULT OF THE OLD DEBT MONETARY SYSTEM, WHICH WAS ONE OF GROW (INFLATE) OR DIE.

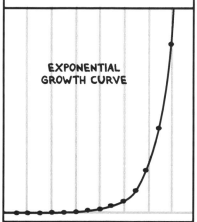

EXPONENTIAL GROWTH CURVE

THE NEW GOAL IS FOR PEOPLE TO HAVE EVERYTHING THEY NEED TO LIVE COMFORTABLY USING THE LEAST AMOUNT OF TIME AND ENERGY--AND THUS THE LEAST AMOUNT OF MONEY.

PRICES FOR MOST THINGS ARE DEFLATIONARY. THAT MEANS THEY CONSISTENTLY GO DOWN. THE GOAL IS FOR THINGS TO COST AS CLOSE TO NOTHING AS POSSIBLE.

ESSENTIALLY, IF YOU WANT TO GET A LOT OF FUNDING FOR A BUSINESS THROUGH THE STOCK MARKET, THE GOAL OF YOUR BUSINESS NEEDS TO BE TO MAKE A PRODUCT THAT WILL END UP AS CLOSE TO FREE AS POSSIBLE. IF IT DOES OTHERWISE, IT IS DOOMED TO FAIL AS COMPETITION DESTROYS THE ARTIFICIAL SCARCITY IT TRIES TO MAINTAIN.

PEOPLE ARE REWARDED FOR ADVANCING EFFICIENCY NOT PERPETUATING SCARCITY.

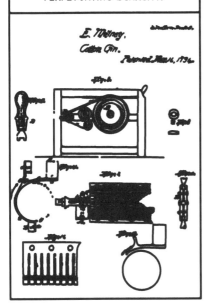

ONCE A PUBLICLY TRADED COMPANY BECOMES PROFITABLE, IT USUALLY STARTS TO BUY UP ITS OWN SHARES UNTIL IT BECOMES PRIVATE. THAT'S THE STANDARD WAY OF OPERATING THESE DAYS. OTHERWISE, THE COMPANY IS CAUGHT IN THE TRAP OF HAVING TO USE GIMMICKS TO GROW THE SHARE PRICE AND APPEASE SHAREHOLDERS.

BUSINESSES IN VOLUNTARY SOCIETY ARE MORE RESPECTED BY CUSTOMERS WHEN THE PEOPLE WHO ACTUALLY WORK IN THE COMPANY CALL THE SHOTS AND KEEP ALL THE PROFITS AND LIABILITY. THEN THE COMPANY CAN THINK RESPONSIBLY LONG-TERM INSTEAD OF SIMPLY ABOUT HOW TO GET THE STOCK PRICE UP IN A POINTLESS MARCH TO EVENTUAL OBLIVION.

WE NEED TO INCREASE PROFITS TO KEEP THE SHARE PRICE RISING. LET'S RAISE PRICES. SURE IT MIGHT CAUSE A CUSTOMER REVOLT THAT LEADS TO THE BANKRUPTCY OF THE COMPANY, BUT WE HAVE NO CHOICE EXCEPT GROW OR DIE.

THE STOCK THAT HAS BEEN ON FIRE LATELY IS THE STOCK OF A COMPANY CALLED TRUE ALCHEMY, WHICH IS TRYING TO DEVELOP TECHNOLOGY THAT WILL TAP INTO QUANTUM VACUUM ENERGY TO REARRANGE SUBATOMIC PARTICLES INTO DIFFERENT ELEMENTS.

TRUE ALCHEMY

DELIVERING A FUTURE OF UNLIMITED ABUNDANCE

THAT MEANS, IF SUCCESSFUL, THEY SHOULD BE ABLE TO EVENTUALLY TURN A PILE OF ASH INTO A PILE OF GOLD OR EVENTUALLY EVEN APPLES. THAT'S NEARLY THE HOLY GRAIL OF ECONOMIC PROGRESS.

THEY KEEP ON SHOWING ENOUGH PROGRESS TO KEEP PEOPLE BUYING STOCK. WE'LL SEE IF THEY SUCCEED OR FAIL, BUT PEOPLE OBVIOUSLY SEE IT AS A WORTHY GAMBLE. AND I DOUBT THEY ARE LYING ABOUT THEIR FINDINGS, BECAUSE IF SO, THEY ARE INEVITABLY SCREWED.

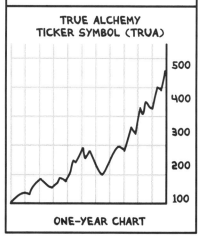

TRUE ALCHEMY
TICKER SYMBOL (TRUA)

500

400

300

200

100

ONE-YEAR CHART

WELL, I DON'T WANT TO LINGER AND DISTRACT YOU. WHAT TIME DO YOU PLAN ON BEING HOME?

ABOUT ONE.

COOL, I'LL CERTAINLY BE DONE WITH MY FRIEND BY THEN.

WHAT ELSE DO YOU WANT TO SEE? LET'S GO NEXT DOOR TO LOOK AT THE TAN TACO STAND.

PEANYWIS

SEE HOW THIS RESTAURANT IS APPROVED BY THESE THREE RESTAURANT QUALITY ASSURERS? YOU KNOW YOU'RE GETTING GOOD STUFF HERE. APPROVAL MEANS THE INGREDIENTS AND FOOD PREPARATION CONDITIONS ARE ALL HIGH QUALITY.

ORGANIC WISE
A 07-07 A 08-22 A 10-01

QUALITY EXPERTS
A 07-04 A 08-16 A 9-23

DINERS CHOICE
A 06-25 A 08-02 A 10-04

ALSO, SEE THE GRADES AND DATES OF THE THREE MOST RECENT SURPRISE INSPECTIONS BY THESE QUALITY ASSURERS?

EVEN OUR TACO STANDS ARE REALLY NICE, BECAUSE YOU CAN'T GET AWAY WITH POOR QUALITY. AND THAT'S REALLY TRUE OF JUST ABOUT ANYTHING YOU CAN BUY.

THE TAN TAC

ORGANIC WISE
A 07-07 A 08-22 A 10-01

QUALITY EXPERTS
A 07-04 A 08-16 A 9-23

DINERS CHOICE
A 06-25 A 08-02 A 10-04

138

THERE ISN'T JUST SOME FLUNKY GOVERNMENT ORGANIZATION EVERYONE IS ASSUMING IS KEEPING PEOPLE SAFE FROM POOR QUALITY. PEOPLE ACTUALLY HAVE TO DO SOME HOMEWORK AND SEE HOW REPUTATIONS STACK UP.

THERE ARE MANY QUALITY ASSURANCE COMPANIES OUT THERE. AND THEY ALL NEED TO KEEP A GOOD REPUTATION OF ASSURING TRUE QUALITY IN ORDER TO STAY IN BUSINESS.

WHERE ELSE SHOULD WE GO? WE COULD GO SEE MY BROTHER WHO WORKS ON RESEARCH AND MODELING FOR A WEATHER FORECASTING BUSINESS. WITH NO MORE GOVERNMENT-FUNDED WEATHER, ACCURATE WEATHER DATA IS EXTRA BIG BUSINESS.

BUT THAT WOULD BE KIND OF A LONG DRIVE JUST TO SEE A BUNCH OF PEOPLE WORKING ON COMPUTERS.

SO ANYWAY, I THINK WE'VE SEEN ENOUGH. YOU GET THE POINT. THIS IS JUST SPECULATION OF ONE WAY SOCIETY COULD ORGANIZE UNDER VOLUNTARYISM.

IF VOLUNTARYISM AROSE DUE TO SOMETHING LIKE TECHNOLOGY, AS OPPOSED TO THE LOGICAL MORAL ARGUMENT FOR VOLUNTARYISM, THEN A VOLUNTARYIST WORLD COULD LOOK MUCH DIFFERENT FROM THE ONE I JUST DESCRIBED.

JUST IMAGINE IF SOMEONE INVENTED SOME KIND OF PERSONAL FORCE FIELD SYSTEM. YOU COULD WALK AROUND AND INTERACT WITH PEOPLE WITHOUT ANY DANGER OF ANYONE BEING ABLE TO INITIATE FORCE UPON YOU.

YOU COULD ALSO PROTECT YOUR PROPERTY WITH A FORCE FIELD.

THAT'S THE KIND OF THING THAT MIGHT MAKE PEOPLE LOSE INTEREST IN GOVERNMENT REGARDLESS OF THE MORAL ARGUMENT AGAINST GOVERNMENT.

WE DON'T NEED NO STINKIN' STATE!

FRANKLY, OTHER THAN ISOLATED POCKETS OF VOLUNTARYISM, IT IS UNLIKELY WE'LL SEE WIDESPREAD VOLUNTARYISM ARISE WITHOUT THE SUPPORT OF TECHNOLOGY. THEREFORE, TECHNOLOGY IS VITAL.

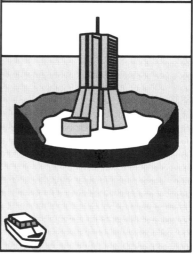

TECHNOLOGICAL ADVANCEMENT TRUMPS POLITICAL ACTION ANY DAY. SO, IF YOU REALLY WANT A FREE WORLD, GET INVENTING!

NONETHELESS, THE MORAL ARGUMENT FOR VOLUNTARYISM LOGICALLY STANDS ON ITS OWN REGARDLESS OF ANYTHING ELSE.

TRUTH

NOLICENSE

SEE YOU IN THE NEXT CHAPTER.

CHAPTER SIX

WHAT IS TRUTH?

OKAY, IT'S TIME TO COVER SOME TERRITORY FEW WOULD EXPECT FROM A BOOK LIKE THIS. I'M GOING TO GET VERY HEAVY, ABSTRACT, AND PHILOSOPHICAL. SO, BEAR WITH ME, BECAUSE THIS IS A WORTHWHILE THOUGHT EXPERIMENT. IF YOU'VE BEEN OPEN MINDED ENOUGH TO STICK WITH ME SO FAR, I HOPE YOU'LL BE OPEN MINDED ENOUGH TO STICK WITH ME THROUGH THIS CHAPTER.

WHAT I WANT TO DO IS CONTEMPLATE HOW THE NON-AGGRESSION PRINCIPLE APPLIES TO THE BIGGER PICTURE AND ULTIMATELY TO TRUTH.

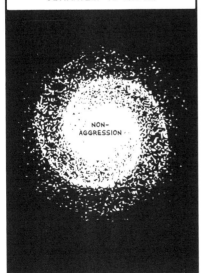

NON-AGGRESSION

IT COULD EASILY BE SAID THAT A LIE IS ESSENTIALLY THE INITIATION OF FORCE ON TRUTH. IGNORANCE IS NOT REALLY AN INITIATION OF FORCE ON TRUTH. HOWEVER, WHEN IGNORANCE IS PRESENTED AS TRUTH, THEN IT IS INDEED AN INITIATION OF FORCE ON TRUTH.

LIE

TRUTH

GOVERNMENT IS A PRIME EXAMPLE OF IGNORANCE PRESENTED AS TRUTH. JUST ABOUT EVERYTHING GOVERNMENT DOES IS IGNORANCE PRESENTED AS TRUTH. GOVERNMENT SAYS THAT IT KNOWS THE SOLUTION. BUT IT ALMOST NEVER REALLY DOES.

YOU GOING 10MPH OVER THE ARBITRARY SPEED LIMIT IS DANGEROUS AND DESERVES A TICKET.

BUT US PURSUING A DIRT BAG IN A STOLEN CAR AT HIGH SPEEDS ENDANGERING HUNDREDS OF PEOPLE MAKES SENSE.

AFTER ALL, TRUTH DOESN'T CONTRADICT ITSELF, BUT GOVERNMENT IS A WALKING CONTRADICTION. GOVERNMENT SAYS:

FORCE IS WRONG, FORCE IS JUST.

GOVERNMENT IS SOMETIMES TRUE ENOUGH TO GET THE JOB OF HUMAN ORGANIZATION DONE, BUT CERTAINLY NOT THE END ALL OF HOW TO GET THE JOB DONE.

KEEP

RIGHT

ALL TRUTH IN THIS WORLD IS ONLY EVER TRUE ENOUGH. NO ONE KNOWS EVERYTHING. AND TO BE ABLE TO CLAIM ABSOLUTE TRUTH YOU'D HAVE TO KNOW EVERYTHING.

THE REALITY IS THAT ABSOLUTE TRUTH IS ELUSIVE IN THIS UNIVERSE. THAT'S WHAT THE MATH SAYS ANYWAY.

IN 1931, AUSTRIAN MATHEMATICIAN KURT GÖDEL PUBLISHED SOMETHING CALLED THE INCOMPLETENESS THEOREM.[7]

THE INCOMPLETENESS THEOREM:

ARITHMETIC IS NOT COMPLETELY FORMALIZABLE. FOR EVERY CONSISTENT FORMALIZATION OF ARITHMETIC, THERE EXIST ARITHMETIC TRUTHS THAT ARE NOT PROVABLE WITHIN THAT FORMAL SYSTEM.

GÖDEL'S DISCOVERY DEMONSTRATED THAT ANY CONSISTENT FORMAL FRAMEWORK USED TO SPEAK ABOUT THE TRUTH OR FALSITY OF MATHEMATICAL STATEMENTS MUST REFERENCE ITSELF, RENDERING IT DOOMED TO INCOMPLETENESS.

A GENERIC FORMAL SYSTEM
IN LOGIC SPACE

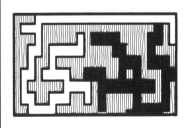

☐ PROVED ■ DISPROVED ▦ UNKNOWABLE

IN THE BIG PICTURE, GÖDEL'S DISCOVERY MEANS THAT WHEN WE TRY TO STUDY THIS UNIVERSE AND SUM IT UP INTO A NICE LITTLE MODEL, WHATEVER MODEL WE COME UP WITH MUST BE AT LEAST SELF-CONTRADICTING AND MOST LIKELY ALSO DOWNRIGHT INCOMPLETE.

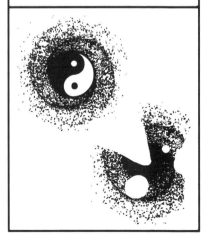

CONSEQUENTLY, IN THIS UNIVERSE, WE ARE LIMITED TO THE TRUE ENOUGH. THAT MEANS AN ENTERPRISE LIKE SCIENCE WILL BE FOREVER PROVISIONAL AND CONSTANTLY BUILD UPON THE TRUE ENOUGH.

FOR EXAMPLE, NEWTON'S EQUATIONS FOR FIGURING OUT MOTION WERE TRUE ENOUGH AND THEY ARE STILL TRUE ENOUGH FOR MOST APPLICATIONS TODAY.

BUT NEWTON'S UNIVERSE WAS A UNIVERSE THAT AMOUNTED TO BUMPING BILLIARD BALLS.

WITH THE DISCOVERIES OF EINSTEIN AND QUANTUM MECHANICS, NEW AND MORE PRECISE EQUATIONS WERE DEVISED THAT SHOWED THE TRUER UNIVERSE IS STRANGER THAN THE BUMPING BILLIARD BALLS OF NEWTON'S UNIVERSE.

AND IT IS SAFE TO SAY THAT THE WAY PHYSICS VIEWS THE UNIVERSE TODAY WILL EVENTUALLY GIVE WAY TO YET AN EVEN TRUER PICTURE. THAT PICTURE MAY BLUDGEON MANY OF THE IDEAS THAT PEOPLE TODAY ALIGNED WITH THE SCIENTIFIC PURSUIT OF TRUTH HOLD ONTO AS EMPIRICAL AND SELF-EVIDENT.

IN CASE YOU'VE NEVER NOTICED, YOU'VE NEVER REALLY EXPERIENCED THE WORLD. ALL YOU'VE EVER SEEN OF THE WORLD IS A PICTURE IN YOUR MIND.

IN THE UNIVERSE OF A HUMAN BEING, MIND IS THE CENTER: MIND IS PRIMARY. YET, WE TEND TO LOOK OUT INTO THE WORLD AND SAY THAT IT IS REAL, NOT MIND.

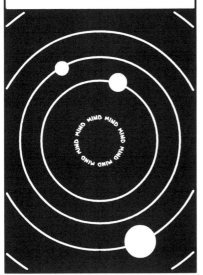

BUT LET ME ASK YOU THIS: WHAT SEEMS MORE IMPLAUSIBLE, THAT ARRANGING MATTER IN A CERTAIN WAY (WHATEVER MATTER IS) MAKES A MIND OR THAT MIND IS ACTUALLY MORE PRIMARY THAN MATTER?

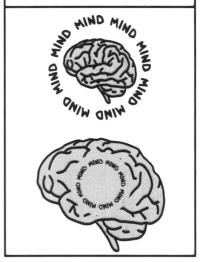

AFTER ALL, I AM TALKING TO A MIND RIGHT NOW.

I DON'T KNOW ABOUT YOU, BUT THERE IS ONLY ONE WAY I KNOW OF FIRST HAND TO MAKE A UNIVERSE: DREAM IT. EVERY NIGHT WHEN I GO TO BED, I MAKE UP AN ENTIRE UNIVERSE IN MY MIND.

MY DREAM WORLDS OFTEN SEEM MUCH LIKE THIS WORLD, EXCEPT THE PHYSICAL LAWS OF MY DREAM WORLDS ARE OFTEN MUCH MORE FLEXIBLE.

MY DREAM WORLDS ARE POPULATED WITH SEEMINGLY SEPARATE PEOPLE, PLANTS, BUILDINGS, YOU NAME IT. YET, IT IS ALL JUST A PROJECTION OF MY OWN MIND.

SO, LET ME ASK YOU THIS: WOULD IT MAKE SENSE FOR ME TO KEEP MYSELF ASLEEP AND DREAMING SO I COULD SCIENTIFICALLY STUDY WHAT IS TRUE IN MY DREAMS?

OF COURSE NOT, BECAUSE BY WAKING UP I'D DISCOVER THAT MY DREAMS WERE ONLY EVER TRUE TO ME.

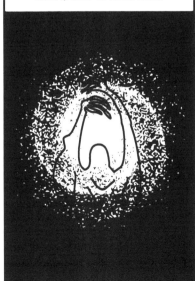

WELL, WHO'S TO SAY THAT THIS ENTIRE UNIVERSE ISN'T JUST A DREAM? WHO'S TO SAY IT ISN'T A GHOST, LIKE GOVERNMENT?

THAT WOULD MEAN THAT WHEN WE STUDY THE UNIVERSE IN SEARCH OF THE TRUTH, ALL WE ARE DOING IS LOOKING AT THE SUBJECTIVE PROJECTIONS OF OUR OWN COLLECTIVE MIND.

TIME AND SPACE: SELF-DECEIVING TRICKS TO DISASSOCIATE OURSELVES FROM OURSELVES.

JUST AS YOUR MIND IS BEHIND EVERYTHING PROJECTED INSIDE ONE OF YOUR INDIVIDUAL DREAMS, PERHAPS THE SAME IS TRUE OF THE UNIVERSE.

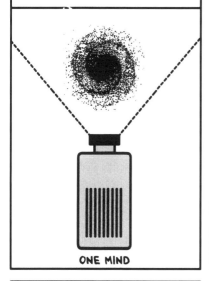

ONE MIND

PERHAPS THE PERSON YOU CALL YOURSELF IS REALLY JUST A DISASSOCIATED FRAGMENT OF THE SAME MIND BEHIND EVERYONE AND EVERYTHING ELSE IN THIS UNIVERSE.

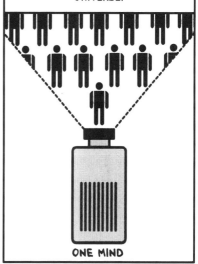

ONE MIND

THAT WOULD MEAN THAT WHO YOU REALLY ARE IS THE SAME AS WHO I REALLY AM: **THE DREAMER OF THE DREAM**. HAVE YOU EVER CONTEMPLATED SUCH AN IDEA? IF YOU HAVEN'T, IT IS PROBABLY A BIT DISTURBING.

BECAUSE IT MEANS THAT ALL THOSE JERKS THAT YOU HATE OR JUST DON'T LIKE OUT THERE ARE REALLY JUST DISASSOCIATED FRAGMENTS OF YOUR ULTIMATE **ONE** SELF: THE MIND DREAMING THIS UNIVERSE.

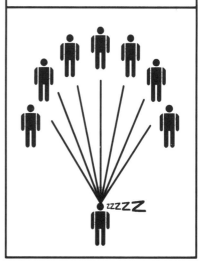

149

AND IF THOSE SEEMINGLY OTHER PEOPLE AND THINGS OUT THERE ARE GUILTY BASTARDS, THEN YOU ARE A GUILTY BASTARD YOURSELF. WHICH WOULD MEAN THAT THE VOLUNTARYIST PRINCIPLE OF NON-AGGRESSION WOULD BE EVEN MORE WARRANTED ON A PSYCHOLOGICAL LEVEL THAN THE PHYSICAL LEVEL.

THEREFORE, MAYBE A GUY LIKE JESUS WASN'T A DELUDED PSYCHOTIC, OR A GUY INTERESTED IN STARTING THE ECLECTIC RELIGION THAT FALLS UNDER THE UMBRELLA KNOWN AS CHRISTIANITY.

I WAS WAY AHEAD OF MY TIME 2000 YEARS AGO AND I STILL AM.

MAYBE HE WAS JUST A GUY THAT ACTUALLY WOKE UP BY APPLYING THE NON-AGGRESSION PRINCIPLE PSYCHOLOGICALLY WITHOUT COMPROMISE.

IF WE ARE TO BELIEVE THE DESCRIPTIONS FOUND IN THE BIBLE OF WHAT JESUS TAUGHT, HE CERTAINLY SEEMS TO HAVE BEEN A FAN OF THE NON-AGGRESSION PRINCIPLE APPLIED BOTH PHYSICALLY AND PSYCHOLOGICALLY.

DO UNTO OTHERS AS YOU WOULD HAVE OTHERS DO UNTO YOU.

OVERALL, JUST AS THE NON-AGGRESSION PRINCIPLE RENDERS GOVERNMENT NOTHING MORE THAN A NIGHTMARE, PERHAPS IT DOES THE SAME TO THE ENTIRE UNIVERSE.

THAT WOULD MEAN THAT THE UNIVERSE IS LIKE THE GOVERNMENT; IT IS A FICTION THAT TRIES TO KEEP A SELF-CONTRADICTING FALSEHOOD SEEMINGLY REAL.

FORCE IS WRONG, FORCE IS JUST.

UNTRUTH IS UNREAL, UNTRUTH IS REAL.

IN OTHER WORDS, THE UNIVERSE IS PERHAPS JUST A BIG LIE. LIES AREN'T REAL AND NEITHER ARE DREAMS, THUS DREAMS ARE THE WAY LIES ARE MADE SEEMINGLY TRUE.

TRUE

LIE

THAT LEADS US TO THE QUESTION POSED BY THIS CHAPTER: WHAT IS TRUTH? WELL, FIRST OFF, WE SHOULD LOOK AT THE BEST TOOL HUMANS CURRENTLY HAVE FOR DETERMINING TRUTH: SCIENCE.

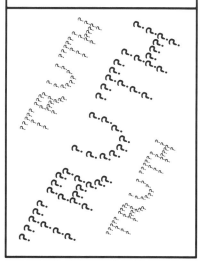

SCIENCE FIGURES OUT WHAT IS TRUE, OR MORE ACCURATELY TRUE ENOUGH, BY BASICALLY FIGURING OUT WHAT IS UNIFIED. AND WHAT IS UNIFIED IN THE SCIENTIFIC SENSE IS THAT WHICH ALL OF OUR MINDS CAN AGREE UPON DUE TO THE CRITERIA OF CONSISTENT EXPERIMENTAL RESULTS.

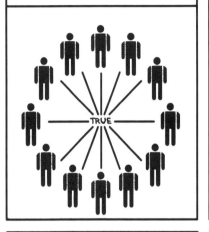

WHAT IS SCIENTIFICALLY TRUE IS THAT WHICH IS BEYOND THE SUBJECTIVE DREAMS OF OUR INDIVIDUAL MINDS. THAT MEANS SCIENCE IS THE STUDY OF WHAT THE DREAM OF OUR **COLLECTIVE MIND** IS: THE ONE FRAGMENTED MIND BEHIND HUMANS, PLANTS, ALIENS, ANIMALS, ROCKS, STARS, ATOMS, AND EVERYTHING ELSE.

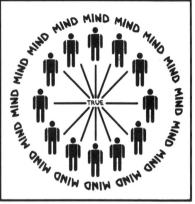

IF WE TAKE THE SCIENTIFIC SENSE OF TRUTH TO THE EXTREME, WE CAN DEFINE ULTIMATE TRUTH AS THAT WHICH IS COMPLETELY UNIFIED, WHOLE, AND ONE, WITHOUT OPPOSITES OR CONTRADICTIONS.

THUS, IN THE DREAM MODEL OF THE UNIVERSE, TRUTH IS MIND IN A STATE OF PERFECT UNIFICATION: ONENESS. THAT PERFECT STATE OF MENTAL UNIFICATION IS PERHAPS WHAT IDEAS LIKE HEAVEN AND NIRVANA POINT TO. PERHAPS HEAVEN IS NOT JUST A FANTASY BUT A REAL STATE OF MIND THAT CERTAIN HUMANS HAVE ACTUALLY EXPERIENCED THROUGHOUT HISTORY.

IN THE DREAM MODEL OF THE UNIVERSE, MIND STARTS OUT IN A UNIFIED STATE OF PERFECT TRUTH. WHAT MIND DOES EXACTLY IN A STATE OF PERFECT TRUTH IS HARD TO FATHOM. TO FATHOM IT WOULD BE TO MODEL IT. AND TO MODEL IT WOULD BE TO MAKE A DOUBLE OF IT. TO MAKE A DOUBLE OF IT WOULD BE TO SPLIT IT AND THUS IT WOULD NO LONGER BE A UNIFIED STATE OF PERFECT TRUTH.

IN THAT SENSE, MODELS ARE LIES: UNTRUE FACSIMILES. ANYTHING THAT CAN BE MODELED IS THUS ILLUSORY. AN ATTEMPT TO MODEL MIND IN A UNIFIED STATE OF PERFECT TRUTH IS THE GENESIS OF UNTRUTH. HENCE, IN THE DREAM MODEL OF THE UNIVERSE, TRYING TO MODEL TRUTH WAS THE GENESIS OF THIS UNIVERSE.

SO, JUST FOR FUN, LET'S BRIEFLY LOOK STEP BY STEP AT HOW WE COULD GO FROM TRUTH TO LIES AND THUS DREAM UP A UNIVERSE.

THE FIRST THING WE NEED TO KEEP IN MIND IS THAT A LIE IS A LIE. AND DUE TO ITS UNREALITY, A LIE HAS NO INFLUENCE ON TRUTH. ONCE A UNIFIED MIND IMAGINES SOMETHING OTHER THAN A UNIFIED STATE OF PERFECT TRUTH, IT MAKES UP AN ILLUSORY SENSE OF SEPARATION. IT MAKES UP THE IDEA OF TWO MINDS RATHER THAN ONE.

THE IDEA OF TWO MINDS IS THE IDEA OF SEPARATION AND THUS THE IDEA OF PRIVACY. SO, WE COULD SAY THE DREAM ALL STARTED WITH A SEPARATE SENSE OF MIND ENTERTAINING THE PRIVATE IDEA OF SEPARATION WHILE THE MIND AS A WHOLE CONTINUED ON AS IF NOTHING HAPPENED. THE LIE COULDN'T BE SHARED AND THUS IT COULDN'T BE MADE TRUE SINCE TRUTH IS PERFECT UNITY.

CONSEQUENTLY, A SEEMINGLY NEW MIND STARTED TO DREAM A DREAM OF SEPARATION FROM THE MIND AS A WHOLE (TRUTH). THE SEEMINGLY NEW MIND WAS THUS PRESENTED WITH THE IDEA OF CHOICE. THERE IS NO CHOICE IN PERFECT UNITY BUT THERE IS CHOICE IN DISUNITY. THEREFORE, THE FIRST CHOICE WAS:

ONCE THE NEW SENSE OF SEPARATE MIND DECIDED TO ENTERTAIN THE IDEA OF UNTRUTH, THERE WAS NO TURNING BACK; IT HAD TO ENTERTAIN THE IDEA UNTIL THE IDEA WAS COMPLETELY EXHAUSTED. SO, THE NEW MIND SEEMINGLY SPLIT ITSELF FROM THE WHOLE MIND AND STARTED TAKING UNTRUTH SERIOUSLY, THUS UNTRUTH STARTED TO SEEM REAL.

THE NEW MIND STARTED TO BELIEVE THAT IT **AGGRESSED** (WHICH IS A NEW CONCEPT TO THE MIND) AGAINST TRUTH AND DESTROYED TRUTH BY LYING. WITH THAT CAME THE GENESIS OF THE PSYCHOLOGICAL SENSE OF TIME. THERE WAS NOW A PAST OF TRUTH, A PRESENT OF UNTRUTH, AND A FUTURE WHERE TRUTH WILL RETURN.

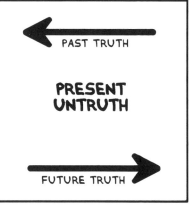

THE FUTURE OF TRUTH RETURNING IS A GOOD THING, BUT THE NEW MIND STARTED TO GO NUTS BECAUSE WHERE ONCE EVERYTHING WAS GOOD AND POSITIVE IN TRUTH, IN LIES EVERY GOOD THING STARTED TO HAVE AN OPPOSITE. THEREFORE, THE MIND STARTED TO SEE THE FUTURE OF TRUTH RETURNING AS TRUTH RETURNING TO AGGRESS AGAINST THE LIE.

THE NEW MIND THUS STARTED TO FEAR THE TRUTH, WHICH WAS NOW SEEMINGLY SEPARATE, AND THE NEW MIND ASCRIBED TO THE TRUTH THE VERY SELF-CONTRADICTING AGGRESSION THAT WAS THE ILLUSORY GENESIS OF UNTRUTH TO BEGIN WITH.

CONSCIOUSNESS IN THE DREAM MODEL: CONSCIOUSNESS IS THE MIND AS A PERCEIVER. TO PERCEIVE REQUIRES AT LEAST TWO THINGS, AN OBSERVER AND OBSERVED. CONSCIOUSNESS IS THUS THE MIND SPLIT. TRUTH IS NOT MULTIPLICITY, THEREFORE MIND IN TRUTH WOULD BE BEING, NOT CONSCIOUSNESS.

AS THE NEW MIND DESCENDED FURTHER INTO MADNESS, THINGS BECAME UNBEARABLE. THE NEW MIND WAS AFRAID TO GO BACK TO TRUTH BUT ALSO AFRAID OF TRUTH FINDING THE LIE AND DESTROYING IT. THE NEW MIND BEGAN TO BELIEVE THAT:

IF THE LIE IS NOT REAL, I AM NOT REAL...I AM DESTROYED.

THUS, THE DELUDED NEW MIND NEEDED TO GET AS FAR AWAY FROM TRUTH AS POSSIBLE, WHICH MEANT THE NEW MIND NEEDED TO GET OUT OF THE MIND. THE NEW MIND THUS DEVISED A WAY TO LIVE WITH THE LIE WITHOUT LIVING WITH THE TERRIFYING SENSE OF FEAR THAT CAME WITH BEING RESPONSIBLE FOR THE LIE.

THE NEW MIND THUS SPLIT ITSELF TO MAKE MOST OF THE MIND UNCONSCIOUS. THEN THE NEW MIND PROJECTED THE UNCONSCIOUS MIND OUT TO MAKE THE UNIVERSE. IN THE DREAM MODEL, THE BIG BANG WAS THUS THE BIG PROJECTION. THEREFORE, WHAT WE THINK OF AS ENERGY/MATTER IS ESSENTIALLY JUST PROJECTED THOUGHT.

SO, THE FINAL INGREDIENT WAS THE PHYSICAL UNIVERSE OF PROJECTED THOUGHT SEPARATED BY SPACE/TIME. THE NEW MIND DILUTED ITSELF INTO COUNTLESS FRAGMENTS AND THOSE COUNTLESS FRAGMENTS ARE CURRENTLY EXPERIENCING THE UNIVERSE THROUGH COUNTLESS BODIES. ALL OF THOSE BODIES LIMIT THE MIND TO KEEP IT ASLEEP AND SEEMINGLY SAFE FROM THE TRUTH. BODIES ALLOW THE SPLIT MIND TO PRETEND THAT IT IS THE DREAM AND NOT THE DREAMER.

IN THE DREAM MODEL, THE UNIVERSE IS BASICALLY JUST AN EXTRAPOLATION OF THE SEEMING INITIATION OF FORCE ON TRUTH. THEREFORE, THE UNIVERSE IS NATURALLY A PLACE OF KILL OR BE KILLED.

THE UNIVERSE IS JUST AN ELABORATE WAR OF THE SELF AGAINST THE SELF, WHEREBY EACH FRAGMENT OF MIND IS ATTEMPTING TO LAY THE BLAME FOR THE ABANDONMENT OF TRUTH ON SOME OTHER FRAGMENT OF MIND.

MY HANDS ARE CLEAN. IT'S THE GLOVE! THE GLOVE DID IT! THE ALMIGHTY GLOVE!

THAT BLAME GAME KEEPS THE LIE SEEMINGLY ALIVE AND IT IS NOT ONLY REFLECTED IN OUR PSYCHOLOGY BUT ALSO IN THE PHYSICAL ATTRIBUTES OF THE UNIVERSE.

THE UNIVERSE IS BASICALLY A BIG MACHINE FEEDING OFF ITSELF. AS IT FEEDS OFF ITSELF, IT GENERATES POCKETS OF ORDER AT THE COST OF AN OVERALL INCREASE OF ENTROPY. ENTROPY IS A MEASUREMENT OF THE AMOUNT OF ENERGY NOT AVAILABLE TO DO WORK IN A SYSTEM. ENTROPY IS THE ARROW OF TIME.

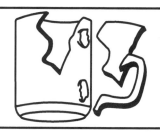

THAT'S .WHY IT IS A LOT EASIER TO BREAK A MUG THAN MAKE A MUG OR PUT A BROKEN MUG BACK TOGETHER. DESTRUCTION IS A REPETITION OF THE ILLUSION OF THE DESTRUCTION OF TRUTH.

THE HUMAN BODY IS A POCKET OF ORDER. BUT AS WE ALL KNOW, THAT POCKET OF ORDER EVENTUALLY GIVES WAY TO ENTROPY AND DIES. TO MAINTAIN THE HUMAN BODY, IT MUST KEEP IN **DISEQUILIBRIUM** WITH ITS ENVIRONMENT. IT DOES THAT THROUGH METABOLISM: CONSUMING SUBSTANCES.

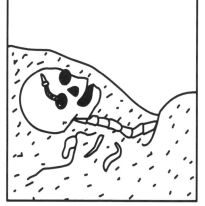

WE BREATHE, EAT, DRINK, AND WE ALSO KEEP OUR BODIES IN SUITABLE TEMPERATURES. TO STAY ALIVE, WE HAVE TO INITIATE FORCE ON PLANTS OR ANIMALS. HOWEVER, NOT ALL OUR FEEDING IS BLATANTLY KILL OR BE KILLED: CONSUME OR BE CONSUMED.

THERE ARE SOME SYMBIOTIC RELATIONSHIPS OF WIN-WIN LIKE HUMANS GENERATING CO_2 FROM OXYGEN AND PLANTS GENERATING OXYGEN FROM CO_2.

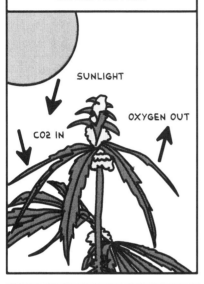

SUNLIGHT

OXYGEN OUT

CO2 IN

BUT ULTIMATELY, WE ARE FOR THE MOST PART ALL FEEDING OFF THE ENERGY REACHING EARTH FROM THE SUN AND PREVIOUS SUNS THAT GENERATED THE HEAVIER ELEMENTS THAT MAKE UP EARTH.

OVER TIME, ENTROPY INCREASES EVERMORE AS THE UNIVERSE SEEKS AN EQUILIBRIUM OF MAXIMAL ENTROPY. MAXIMAL ENTROPY REPRESENTS A KIND OF THEORETICAL UNITY ON THE BACKSIDE OF UNTRUTH. WHEN THE DREAMER HAS COMPLETELY CONSUMED ITSELF, THE DREAMER HAS EXHAUSTED THE LIE: THERE ARE NO DISASSOCIATED FRAGMENTS OF THE SELF LEFT TO FEED UPON.

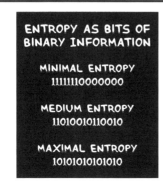

ENTROPY AS BITS OF BINARY INFORMATION

MINIMAL ENTROPY
11111110000000

MEDIUM ENTROPY
11010010110010

MAXIMAL ENTROPY
10101010101010

THE DOWNFALL OF A GOVERNMENT, THE DOWNFALL OF A HUMAN BODY, THE DOWNFALL OF A UNIVERSE; IT CAN BE SEEN AS THE SAME DYNAMIC: THE EXHAUSTION OF THE INITIATION OF FORCE ON THE SELF TO MAINTAIN A FICTION: A LIE OF SEPARATION.

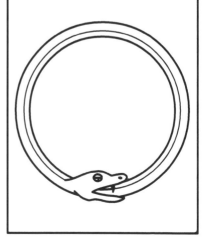

IF YOU COME FROM A TRADITIONAL RELIGIOUS BACKGROUND, BY SUGGESTING THAT THE UNIVERSE IS A DREAM, I'VE BASICALLY JUST SUGGESTED THAT GOD DIDN'T MAKE THIS UNIVERSE. I'VE SAID THIS UNIVERSE IS JUST A BAD IDEA THAT TRIED TO PULL OFF THE IMPOSSIBLE BY MAKING SOMETHING THAT ISN'T TRUTH, ISN'T UNITY.

AND FRANKLY, IF YOU ACTUALLY LOOK AT YOUR OWN RELIGION WITH THIS IDEA IN MIND, YOU'LL LIKELY FIND SOME ALLEGORY FOR IT, LIKE THE PRODIGAL SON IN CHRISTIANITY.

WITH THIS IDEA, I DIDN'T GET RID OF NOTIONS LIKE GOD AND SPIRIT (MIND), I JUST SALVAGED THEM FROM THE JUNK PILE OF SUPERSTITION, POLITICAL MANIPULATION, AND LOGICAL INCONSISTENCY.

THE IDEA THAT MIND IS PRIMARY AND THAT THE UNIVERSE IS ESSENTIALLY A DREAM ALSO SUGGESTS THAT THINGS LIKE REINCARNATION, GHOSTS, PSYCHIC INFORMATION, MIND HEALING, AND OTHER METAPHYSICAL NOTIONS CAN'T JUST BE DISMISSED AS HOKUM. THAT WOULD JUST BE STUFF THAT IS TOO MUCH MIND AND NOT ENOUGH MATTER TO MAKE SENSE OF SCIENTIFICALLY AT THIS POINT IN TIME.

IN THE DREAM MODEL OF THE UNIVERSE, YOU EITHER WAKE UP OR WHEN YOU DIE YOU JUST START DREAMING ANOTHER DREAM AS ANOTHER PERSON IN ANOTHER BODY.

IN FACT, THE PHYSICAL SHOULD PERHAPS BE CALLED METAMENTAL RATHER THAN CALLING NONPHYSICAL CONCEPTS LIKE MIND METAPHYSICAL.

THERE ARE SOME PEOPLE IN THIS WORLD WHO CLAIM TO EXPERIENCE THE METAPHYSICAL FROM TIME TO TIME. BUT OBVIOUSLY, THOSE PEOPLE CAN'T CONTROL OR UNDERSTAND THOSE EXPERIENCES VERY WELL. OTHERWISE, THOSE EXPERIENCES WOULD BE SCIENTIFICALLY VERIFIABLE.

HAVE YOU EVER WONDERED WHY A GHOSTLY APPARITION WOULD BE WEARING CLOTHES? WELL, IN THE DREAM MODEL, CLOTHES ARE JUST AS MUCH A PROJECTION OF MIND AS A BODY IS.

TRYING TO PROVE METAPHYSICAL EXPERIENCES IN THIS WORLD IS LIKE A PERSON BORN DEAF RANDOMLY HEARING TEN SECONDS OF BEETHOVEN'S ODE TO JOY AND THEN TRYING TO EXPLAIN IT TO ANOTHER PERSON DEAF SINCE BIRTH. THE SHARED EXPERIENCE NECESSARY TO VERIFY SUCH AN EPHEMERAL EXPERIENCE IS GREATLY LACKING IN SUCH A SCENARIO.

DA
DA DA
DA DA DA DA
DA DA DA DA
DA DAAA
DA DA

EXTRAORDINARY CLAIMS REQUIRE EXTRAORDINARY EVIDENCE, BUT THAT DOESN'T MAKE THE CLAIMS UNTRUE. PERHAPS THE BEST WAY TO GO DOWN IN HISTORY AS A FOOL IS TO PUBLICLY DEFINE THE BOUNDARIES OF WHAT IS POSSIBLE.

HOW DARE YOU SUGGEST THAT I AM MORE THAN JUST A FANCY ROBOT MADE OF MATTER.

AS TECHNOLOGY HAS ADVANCED TO GATHER EVIDENCE FOR METAPHYSICAL NOTIONS, TECHNOLOGY HAS ALSO ADVANCED TO FAKE SUCH EVIDENCE. CONSEQUENTLY, EXPERIENCE RULES IN SUCH MATTERS AND FORTUNATELY OR UNFORTUNATELY, PERSONAL EXPERIENCE ISN'T GOOD ENOUGH FOR SCIENCE.

THE SCIENTIFIC METHOD IS A WONDERFUL TOOL, BUT IT IS NOT A METATHEORY; IT CAN NOT LAY DOWN JUDGMENT ON EVERYTHING. TO TREAT SCIENCE AS A METATHEORY IS TO ENSLAVE ONESELF TO THE TYRANNY OF WHAT IS POSSIBLE WITHIN THE CONFINES OF THE SCIENTIFIC METHOD.

I'VE PERSONALLY HAD NUMEROUS VERY BLATANT PSYCHIC EXPERIENCES, AND I'VE HAD EVEN MORE NUMEROUS SUBTLE EXPERIENCES. THEREFORE, WHEN PEOPLE TELL ME THERE IS NO SUCH THING AS BEING PSYCHIC I JUST SAY:

SPEAK FOR YOURSELF.

JUST THINK WHAT A GREAT ARGUMENT AGAINST INTELLECTUAL PROPERTY PSYCHIC INFORMATION HAS THE POTENTIAL TO BE.

IF THE UNIVERSE IS A DREAM, THEN ALL MINDS ARE ACTUALLY ONE. THEREFORE, THERE'S NO NEED FOR ANY PHYSICAL EXPLANATION FOR HOW PSYCHIC INFORMATION CAN BE TRANSMITTED THROUGH SPACE AND TIME: SPACE, TIME, AND EVERYTHING SEEMINGLY IN IT ARE ALL JUST PROJECTIONS OF THE SAME ONE MIND.

IN THE DREAM MODEL OF THE UNIVERSE, THE UNIVERSE IS DESIGNED TO KEEP THE MIND ASLEEP AND DREAMING. THEREFORE, IT WOULD COME AS NO SURPRISE THAT IT IS HARD TO PROVE THE REALITY OF THINGS THAT MIGHT MAKE THE DREAMER TAKE MIND MORE SERIOUSLY THAN MATTER.

SCIENCE ITSELF HAS COME TO REALIZE THAT IT DOESN'T QUITE KNOW WHAT COMPOSES MOST OF THE UNIVERSE. THAT MYSTERY SUGGESTS THAT, JUST LIKE OUR INDIVIDUAL MINDS, MOST OF THE UNIVERSE IS HIDDEN IN THE UNCONSCIOUS.

THE UNIVERSE IS COMPOSED OF:

4.6% ORDINARY MATTER
23% DARK MATTER
72% DARK ENERGY

IF THE UNIVERSE IS INDEED A DREAM, ONLY YOUR OWN EXPERIENCE OF WAKING UP WILL EVER PROVE IT TO YOU. YOU WON'T BE ABLE TO RELY ON SCIENTISTS WORKING OFF SOME GOVERNMENT GRANT TO PROVE IT TO YOU.

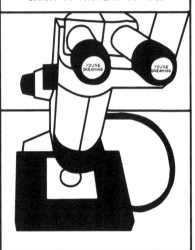

THE WAY YOU WOULD WAKE UP IS BY APPLYING THE MORAL LOGIC OF NON-AGGRESSION MENTALLY. YOU'D WALK THE EARTH ENTERTAINING THE IDEA THAT EVERYONE AND EVERYTHING YOU SEE OUT THERE IS THE SAME MIND AS YOU. YOU WOULD CEASE TO USE FORCE MENTALLY BECAUSE IT WOULD ULTIMATELY BE AN ATTACK ON YOURSELF, KEEPING YOU LOST IN DREAMS.

THAT WOULDN'T MEAN YOU MIGHT NOT HAVE TO PHYSICALLY KICK SOME BUTT IN REACTION TO AN INITIATION OF FORCE ON RARE OCCASION, BUT PSYCHOLOGICALLY YOU WOULDN'T MAKE IT REAL.

THE HYPOTHESIS IS THAT IF YOU STOPPED GIVING REALITY TO UNTRUTH (THAT WHICH IS SELF-CONTRADICTING AND SEPARATE) FOR LONG ENOUGH, YOU'D RELINQUISH YOUR INVESTMENT IN UNTRUTH AND YOU'D WAKE UP TO YOUR TRUE SELF WHICH IS UNIFIED MIND IN TRUTH.

PERFECT UNITY SEEMS BORING.

THAT GOES TO SHOW HOW INCREDIBLY CLUELESS YOU ARE.

THE BUDDHA AND JESUS

THAT'S THE SAME PRINCIPLE BEHIND MOVING AWAY FROM GOVERNMENT TO VOLUNTARYISM. YOU REALIZE THAT THE INITIATION OF FORCE IS NOT ONLY ILLOGICAL, SINCE IT SETS UP THE CONDITIONS FOR FORCE TO BE RECIPROCATED, BUT YOU ALSO UNDERSTAND FORCE IS IMMORAL SINCE IT SPITS IN THE FACE OF TRUTH: TRUTH DEFINED AS THAT WHICH IS UNIFIED AND DOESN'T CONTRADICT ITSELF.

TRUTH

ILLUSION

ONCE YOU DID THAT, YOU'D RELINQUISH YOUR INVESTMENT IN GOVERNMENT. AND ONCE MOST PEOPLE DID THAT, GOVERNMENT COULD NO LONGER EXIST.

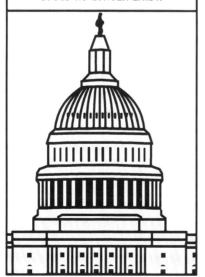

REPLACE PEOPLE WITH THE CONCEPT OF MIND AND THE SAME COULD BE SAID FOR THE ENTIRE UNIVERSE: IT IS A PHANTOM THAT WILL DISAPPEAR WHEN THE MIND STOPS USING FORCE ON ITSELF.

THINKING OF THE UNIVERSE AS A DREAM IS AN EXERCISE THAT AT THE VERY LEAST WORKS TO HELP ONE MORE THOROUGHLY EXPLORE THE CONCEPT OF TRUTH. IT ALSO MAKES A PERSON RECONSIDER COMMON NOTIONS OF CAUSE AND EFFECT.

PEOPLE RAISED IN VIOLENT ENVIRONMENTS TEND TO GROW UP TO BE VIOLENT. BUT IT COULD BE THAT VIOLENT MINDS TEND TO SET UP DREAMS (LIVES) OF VIOLENCE: DREAMS WHERE THE MIND PLAYS OUT VICTIM AND VICTIMIZER ROLES. IN THE DREAM MODEL, VICTIMIZATION IS A MECHANISM FOR KEEPING THE MIND SEEMINGLY SEPARATE FROM OTHER MINDS. THAT SEEMING SEPARATION (MENTAL AGGRESSION) IS WHAT KEEPS THE MIND ASLEEP. CONSEQUENTLY, VIOLENCE COULD ALL BE A BIG SELF-DECEPTION TO KEEP THE MIND ASLEEP. SEEING THROUGH VIOLENCE WOULD BE THE PATH TO AWAKENING.

TRUTH WORTHY OF THE TITLE "**TRUTH**" IS NOT ONLY TRUE SOMETIMES. TRUTH ISN'T VERY TRUE UNLESS IT IS TIMELESS; IT IS ALWAYS TRUE. THAT MEANS THAT ENTERTAINING THE CONCEPT OF UNTRUTH HAS NO INFLUENCE ON REAL TRUTH. TRUTH KNOWS NOTHING OF UNTRUTH. UNTRUTH IS BY DEFINITION AN UNREAL DREAM.

THIS WHOLE CONCEPT OF THE UNIVERSE BEING A DREAM IS AN IDEA, LIKE VOLUNTARYISM, THAT IS OFF THE RADAR SCREEN AND MARGINALIZED. YET, I ASSURE YOU THAT EVEN THOUGH I'VE ONLY COVERED THE SUBJECT BRIEFLY HERE, IT IS A PERFECTLY LOGICAL MODEL, EVEN IF IT DOESN'T FIT WITHIN THE CONFINES OF SCIENCE.

IT ACTUALLY HONORS THE PRIMACY OF THE VERY THING I'M TALKING TO RIGHT NOW, YOUR MIND. AND IT DOES SO WITHOUT DESCENDING INTO A MESS OF SELF-CONTRADICTING HOKUM. YOU CAN'T GET ANY MORE SIMPLE THAN THE IDEA OF ONE THING (ONE UNIFIED MIND IN TRUTH WITHOUT OPPOSITES), EVEN IF IN OUR CONVOLUTED STATE OF MIND SUCH A CONCEPT IS UNFATHOMABLE.

THE FACT IS THAT YOU CANNOT MODEL UNITY/ONE. YOU CANNOT ACCURATELY THINK ABOUT IT, YOU MUST SIMPLY BE IT. THINKING IS MODELING. A MODEL IS ITSELF NOT UNITY AND THUS IS THE DELUSIONAL GENESIS OF UNTRUTH. UNITY IS EITHER A TIMELESS EXPERIENCE OR UNFATHOMABLE SINCE IT CANNOT BE MODELED.

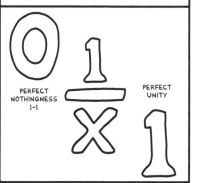

ONE CANNOT BE MODELED AND STILL BE ONE

EVEN THOUGH THE CONCEPT OF PERFECT UNITY IS NECESSARILY METAPHYSICAL, TO SIMPLY DISMISS THE CONCEPT IS TO FALL PREY TO INFINITIES, WHICH ARE ALSO METAPHYSICAL.

3.141592653589793238462643383279502884197
169399375105820974944592307816406286208
998628034825342117067982148086513282306 6
470938446095505822317253594081284811174 5
028410270193852110555964462294895493038 1
964428810975665933446128475648233786783
165271201909145648566923460348610454326 6
482133936072602491412737245870066063155 8
817488152092096282925409171536436789259 0
360011330530548820466521384146951941511 60
944305727036575959195309218611738193261179
310511854807446237996274956735188575272 4
891227938183011949129833673362440656643 08
602139494639522473719070210219860943702 77
053921717629317675238467481846766940513 2
000568127145263560827785771342757788609
173637178721468440901224953430146549585 3
710507922796892589235420199561121290219 60
864034419154981362977047713099605187072 1134
999998372978049951059731732816096318519 50
244594553469083026425223082533446850350 35
261931188171010003137838752886587533200 8381
420617177669147303598253490428755468731 1
595628638823537875937519577818157778053 217
122680661300192787661119590921642019893 80
952572010654858632788659361533818276982 3
030195203530185296899577362259941389124 97

INFINITIES INHABIT A SPACE BETWEEN PERFECT UNITY AND PERFECT NOTHINGNESS. THE MORE YOU SPLIT UP THE CONCEPT OF PERFECT UNITY, THE CLOSER YOU GET TO A HYPOTHETICAL ZERO. IN THAT SENSE, ALL NUMBERS OTHER THAN THE NUMBER ONE AS A WHOLE ARE FRACTIONS. ZERO IS THUS THE QUANTITATIVE EXPRESSION OF WHAT THE RESULT WOULD BE IF UNTRUTH WAS TRUE.

PERFECT NOTHINGNESS
1-1

PERFECT UNITY

THAT MEANS, WE ALL BELIEVE IN EITHER PERFECT UNITY OR INFINITY. THEREFORE, IF, AS EINSTEIN ONCE NOTED, DOING THE SAME THING OVER AND OVER EXPECTING A DIFFERENT RESULT IS THE DEFINITION OF INSANITY, THEN INFINITY IS PURE MADNESS; IT IS AN INSANE DREAM.

GOVERNMENT IS GOOD BUT NOT PERFECT. WE JUST NEED TO KEEP TRYING UNTIL WE GET IT RIGHT.

WITHOUT THE CONCEPT OF PERFECT UNITY, THE SEARCH FOR TRUTH IS PROVISIONAL AND LOST IN MODELS OF MODELS OF MODELS, DREAMS OF DREAMS OF DREAMS, SIMULATIONS OF SIMULATIONS OF SIMULATIONS, UNIVERSES IN UNIVERSES IN UNIVERSES TO INFINITY. IT'S THE LAND OF "NOTHING IS REALLY TRUE" AND "SEEK BUT NEVER REALLY FIND."

LOOKING AT THE WORLD AS A DREAM DOESN'T TRY TO CREATE MIND OUT OF MATTER LIKE SCIENCE OFTEN DOES. YET, IT DOESN'T CONTRADICT SCIENTIFIC OBSERVATION. THE MATERIAL WORLD IS JUST SHOWN AS THE CAGE FOR THE MIND LOST IN LIES. THE MATERIAL WORLD IS A TOOL TO MAKE THE MIND MINDLESS.

BRAIN IS NOT MIND IN THIS MODEL.

BRAIN IS A LIMITATION ON MIND.

IS THE IDEA THAT THE UNIVERSE IS A DREAM TRUE? SINCE IT ISN'T AN IDEA WITHIN THE REALM OF SCIENCE, ONLY YOUR OWN EXPERIENCE COULD EVER TELL YOU. THEREFORE, YOU CAN DO WHATEVER YOU WANT WITH THE IDEA.

ALL I KNOW IS THAT I'M PERSONALLY NOT GOING TO WAIT AROUND FOR SCIENCE TO EXPLAIN TO ME MY VERY OWN EXPERIENCES. TO DO SO WOULD MAKE AS LITTLE SENSE TO ME AS TAKING WHAT SOME ANCIENT DESERT DWELLERS WROTE IN SOME HODGEPODGED BOOK THOUSANDS OF YEARS AGO AS ABSOLUTE TRUTH.

HAMMERS ARE USEFUL TOOLS.

BUT THAT DOESN'T MEAN EVERYTHING IS A NAIL.

YOUR OWN EXPERIENCE IS WHAT IS PRIMARY. BUT YOUR INTERPRETATION OF YOUR OWN EXPERIENCE ISN'T NECESSARILY CORRECT.

JUST ABOUT THE ONLY THING CERTAIN ABOUT WHAT WE KNOW ABOUT THE UNIVERSE IS THAT WHAT WE KNOW IS CONSTANTLY CHANGING. THERE'S NO CLEAR ULTIMATE GOAL.

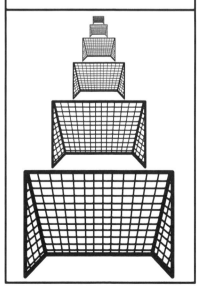

EVERY GOAL MET JUST LEADS TO ANOTHER GOAL. TODAY'S MIND BLOWING DISCOVERY IS TOMORROW'S SO WHAT?

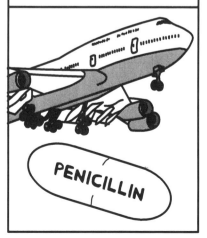

HUMANS INVENT FLIGHT. AFTER AWHILE IT'S LIKE, SO WHAT? HUMANS CURE DISEASES. AFTER AWHILE IT'S LIKE, SO WHAT? AND EVENTUALLY IF HUMANS DO SOMETHING LIKE ESTABLISH UNLIMITED LIFESPAN, IT WILL STILL BE LIKE, SO WHAT?

PENICILLIN

THAT'S WHY I THINK THE DREAM MODEL OF THE UNIVERSE IS WORTH SINCERE CONSIDERATION AND COULD EVENTUALLY PROVE TO BE THE WAVE OF THE FUTURE. IN THE DREAM MODEL, THERE IS AN ULTIMATE GOAL: ONENESS, WHICH IS ALL THAT IS ACTUALLY TRUE.

BUT AS LONG AS YOU CAN ACCEPT THE LOGIC OF NON-AGGRESSION AND VOLUNTARYISM, IT DOESN'T MATTER TO ME WHAT YOU THINK ABOUT THE UNIVERSE BEING A DREAM. SO, DON'T LET THIS MENTAL EXERCISE IN THE NATURE OF TRUTH DISTRACT YOU TOO MUCH FROM WHAT THIS BOOK IS FUNDAMENTALLY ABOUT: NON-AGGRESSION AND VOLUNTARYISM.

MR. VOLUNTARY SAYS:

THE UNIVERSE MAY BE A DREAM, BUT NON-AGGRESSION IS STILL PRACTICAL RIGHT HERE, RIGHT NOW NO MATTER WHAT.

THEREFORE, ALL I CAN SAY IS STAY NIMBLE MY FRIENDS. DON'T START WORSHIPING THE TRUE-ENOUGH AS TRUTH. AND DON'T MISTAKE DREAMS FOR REALITY.

DO YOU CARE ABOUT WHAT IS TRUTH? OR DO YOU PRETEND TO ALREADY KNOW THE TRUTH LIKE A CENTRAL PLANNER FOR THE GOVERNMENT? DO YOU UNDERSTAND WHAT I'M SAYING, OR WON'T YOUR HORNS FIT?

NOTE: DUE TO ITS STRANGENESS AND DEPTH, MOST PEOPLE MAY HAVE TO REREAD THIS CHAPTER REPEATEDLY TO UNDERSTAND AND APPRECIATE IT.

168

CHAPTER SEVEN

FREEDOM IN AN UNFREE WORLD

I REFER BACK TO THE HENRY DAVID THOREAU QUOTE FROM THE BEGINNING OF THE BOOK:

GOVERNMENT IS BEST WHICH GOVERNS NOT AT ALL; AND WHEN MEN ARE PREPARED FOR IT, THAT WILL BE THE KIND OF GOVERNMENT WHICH THEY WILL HAVE.

OBVIOUSLY, HUMANITY IS A FAR CRY FROM BEING PREPARED FOR IT. THE FORCE OF LIES STILL CONTINUES TO PROVE TOO IMPORTANT TO THE POPULACE OF SLAVES.

BUT YOU DON'T HAVE TO WAIT FOR THE REST OF THE SLAVES TO DROP THEIR SHACKLES TO FIND FREEDOM FOR YOURSELF TODAY. WHILE EVERYONE ELSE IS COMPLAINING ABOUT HIS OR HER HORNS NOT FITTING THROUGH THE DOOR, YOU CAN WALK RIGHT THROUGH THE DOOR WITH THE KNOWLEDGE THAT THE HORNS AREN'T REAL.

WAKE UP NOW YOURSELF AND YOU WON'T HAVE TO WAIT FOR EVERYONE ELSE. YOU'LL HAVE STEPPED OUT OF SLAVE TIME.

FIRST OFF, TO BE FREE, YOU MUST BE YOURSELF. IF YOU CAN'T BE YOURSELF AROUND OTHERS, THAT IS INDICATIVE OF SOME KIND OF VICE. THE QUESTION IS, IS THE VICE IN YOU OR THE OTHERS?

IF YOU ARE A THIEF AND YOU CAN'T BE YOUR THIEVING SELF AROUND OTHERS, THEN OBVIOUSLY THE VICE IS IN YOU.

THEFT IS A VICE SINCE IT GOES AGAINST THE NON-AGGRESSION PRINCIPLE. IF YOU ARE A THIEF, OWN UP TO IT AND CHANGE YOUR WAYS. IF YOU DON'T WANT TO CHANGE YOUR WAYS, THEN EVENTUALLY YOU'RE GOING TO STEAL FROM THE WRONG PERSON AND YOUR FORCE WILL BE RECIPROCATED, PERHAPS LETHALLY.

170

CONVERSELY, IF YOU ARE ENTHUSIASTIC ABOUT SOME IDEA, LIKE THAT THE UNIVERSE MIGHT BE A DREAM, BUT KNOW THAT YOU'D GET A BUNCH OF RIDICULE AND REJECTION IF YOU BROUGHT THE IDEA UP TO CERTAIN PEOPLE, THEN THE VICE IS IN THOSE CERTAIN PEOPLE NOT YOURSELF.

MY RELIGION SAYS GOD MADE THE WORLD, NOT A DREAM.

THAT'S NUTTY. IT CAN'T BE PROVEN BY SCIENCE.

YOU CAN CHANGE VICE IN YOURSELF BUT NOT VICE IN OTHERS. BY BEING OPEN ABOUT AN IDEA DEAR TO YOU, LIKE THAT THE UNIVERSE MIGHT BE A DREAM, YOU'LL FIND OUT WHO THE PEOPLE WORTH HAVING RELATIONSHIPS WITH ARE.

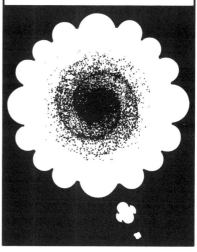

THEY DON'T HAVE TO AGREE WITH YOU, BUT THEY DO NEED TO BE OPEN ENOUGH TO ACCEPT YOU AS YOU ARE.

I REALLY CAN'T ACCEPT THAT WHAT YOU SAY IS RIGHT. BUT THEN AGAIN, I OBVIOUSLY CAN'T SATISFACTORILY CONVINCE YOU TO ACCEPT WHAT I SAY IS RIGHT. THAT'S HOW IT GOES IN A UNIVERSE OF LIMITED INFORMATION.

SUCH AN IDEA WOULD ONLY BECOME VICE IF YOU WENT AROUND INSISTING THAT EVERYONE CHANGE TO THINK LIKE YOU.

IF YOU DON'T HAVE AT LEAST ONE PINT OF THE BLOOD OF CHRIST, YOU ARE GOING TO HELL!

MAYBE YOUR PET IDEA IS RIGHT, BUT IF YOU WANT TO BE FREE, YOU CAN'T WORRY ABOUT CHANGING OTHERS TO THINK LIKE YOU.

IF YOU WANT PEOPLE TO ACCEPT YOU AS YOU ARE, YOU AT LEAST NEED TO ACCEPT OTHER PEOPLE AS THEY ARE. AFTER ALL, INSISTING THAT EVERYONE AGREE WITH YOU IS THE SAME GAME THE GOVERNMENT PLAYS.

AGREE WITH ME OR ELSE!

FACE IT, ALTHOUGH IT MAY BE IDEAL TO SHARE A PASSION FOR AS MANY OF THE SAME THINGS AS POSSIBLE WITH ANOTHER PERSON, SUCH IS CERTAINLY NOT NECESSARY FOR A SATISFYING RELATIONSHIP.

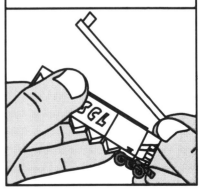

A MAN WHO ENJOYS BUILDING SCALE MODELS OF VINTAGE RAILROAD EQUIPMENT DOESN'T NEED HIS WIFE TO SHARE IN HIS INTEREST IN ORDER TO HAVE A SATISFYING RELATIONSHIP WITH HER. ALL THAT IS REQUIRED OF HIS WIFE IS THAT SHE ACCEPTS THAT HER HUSBAND'S INTERESTS MAKE HIM HAPPY. THUS, SUPPORTING HIS INTERESTS SHOULD IN TURN MAKE HER HAPPY AND VICE VERSA.

BUT YOU HAVE TO DISTINGUISH BETWEEN VIRTUE AND VICE. IF A MAN ENJOYS GETTING DRUNK AND THEN ABUSIVE WITH HIS WIFE, THEN HIS WIFE WOULD BE AN ENSLAVED FOOL TO ACCEPT SUCH VICE FROM HER HUSBAND.

DON'T BE A WIFE BEATER

TO ACCEPT A VIOLATION OF THE SIMPLE LOGIC OF THE NON-AGGRESSION PRINCIPLE IS THE SELF-DEFEATING BEHAVIOR OF A SLAVE.

A FREE PERSON IS LIBERATED BY FOLLOWING THE BASIC MORALITY OF NON-AGGRESSION. MORALITY BEYOND THAT IS SUBJECTIVE.

FOLLOWING THE BASIC MORALITY OF NON-AGGRESSION MEANS:

DO NOT INITIATE FORCE YOURSELF.

DO NOT CONDONE THE INITIATION OF FORCE BY OTHERS.

HOWEVER, NOT INITIATING FORCE YOURSELF DOESN'T JUST APPLY TO NOT INITIATING FORCE ON OTHERS, IT ALSO APPLIES TO NOT INITIATING FORCE ON YOURSELF.

SELF-DESTRUCTIVE BEHAVIOR IS YOUR OWN BUSINESS. BUT IN RELATION TO OTHERS, IT IS VICE NOT VIRTUE. WHETHER THAT SELF-DESTRUCTIVE BEHAVIOR IS SOMETHING LIKE DRUG AND ALCOHOL ABUSE, OR VOLUNTEERING TO RISK LIFE AND LIMB IN A WAR, IN RELATION TO OTHERS, IT IS VICE NOT VIRTUE. AND AS VICE, IT IS NOT LOGICALLY MORAL.

A MAN THAT DOES NOT ACT IN HIS OWN BEST INTEREST CANNOT LOGICALLY BE EXPECTED TO ACT IN THE BEST INTEREST OF ANYONE ELSE.

I'M STINKIN' DRUNK. DO YOU WANT TO GO FOR A DRIVE WITH ME?

YOUR BEST INTEREST IS THE SAME AS MY BEST INTEREST. AND MY BEST INTEREST IS TO HAVE THE FREEDOM TO LIVE IN ANY WAY I WANT AS LONG AS IT IS FREE OF COERCION.

AN ATTACK ON ANOTHER IS INEVITABLY AN ATTACK ON THE SELF--SINCE IT SETS UP PRECEDENCE FOR FORCE BEING ACCEPTABLE.

I'M GLUE AND YOU'RE RUBBER, WHATEVER I BOUNCE OFF YOU STICKS TO ME.

THE SAME APPLIES IN REVERSE: AN ATTACK ON THE SELF IS INEVITABLY AN ATTACK ON ANOTHER SINCE IT SETS UP PRECEDENCE FOR FORCE BEING ACCEPTABLE.

I'M RUBBER AND YOU'RE GLUE, WHATEVER I BOUNCE OFF MYSELF ULTIMATELY HURTS BOTH OF US.

A MAN WILLING TO KILL IN A WAR IS NECESSARILY WILLING TO BE KILLED IN A WAR JUST AS A MAN WILLING TO BE KILLED IN A WAR IS WILLING TO KILL IN A WAR...

...EVEN IF THE ONLY PERSON HE KILLS IS HIMSELF.

SEE WHAT I MEAN? IT IS SIMPLE LOGIC THAT WORKS IN A LOOP BOTH FORWARD AND BACKWARD. THE ONLY WAY OUT OF THE LOOP IS TO SET DOWN THE GUN--SET DOWN THE FORCE.

WHATEVER ANYONE ELSE CALLS MORALITY, IT IS CERTAINLY NOT MORALITY IF IT VIOLATES THE NON-AGGRESSION PRINCIPLE. SO, FOR EXAMPLE, ONE COULD NOT SAY THAT IT IS MORAL TO BE UNSELFISH, BECAUSE ABSENT OF AGGRESSION, THE BEST INTEREST OF THE SELF IS ULTIMATELY THE SAME AS THE BEST INTEREST OF OTHERS.

NOR COULD ONE SIMPLY THEN SAY THAT SELFISHNESS IS MORALITY, BECAUSE AGAIN, ABSENT OF AGGRESSION, THE BEST INTEREST OF OTHERS IS ULTIMATELY THE SAME AS THE BEST INTEREST OF THE SELF. THEREFORE, SELFISHNESS IS ONLY MORAL IF IT DOES NOT VIOLATE THE NON-AGGRESSION PRINCIPLE.

PEOPLE OFTEN LIKE TO DREAM UP ONE IN A BILLION SCENARIOS WHERE THE INITIATION OF FORCE WOULD BE SEEMINGLY JUSTIFIED. AND THEY THEN TRY TO USE SUCH SCENARIOS AS PROOF THAT THE NON-AGGRESSION PRINCIPLE IS NOT UNIVERSAL.

ETHICAL DILEMMA: WHAT DO YOU DO IF A FAT MAN IS STUCK BLOCKING THE EXIT OF A SEASIDE CAVE THUS TRAPPING A GROUP OF PEOPLE WHO WILL DROWN WHEN THE TIDE RISES?

HOWEVER, THERE IS SUCH A THING AS ACCIDENTAL AGGRESSION. AND IN THE CASE OF ACCIDENTAL AGGRESSION, IT IS UP TO THE PEOPLE INVOLVED TO WEIGH THE OPTIONS AND WORK IT OUT.

WE'RE DAMNED IF WE DO AND DAMNED IF WE DON'T.

HOWEVER, I THINK THERE IS ACTUALLY A BACK EXIT TO THE CAVE.

EVERYTHING IN THIS UNIVERSE COMES AT A PRICE. AND TO GET WHAT YOU WANT, YOU HAVE TO BE WILLING TO PAY A PRICE OF SOME KIND. THERE AREN'T REALLY ANY WIN-LOSE TRANSACTIONS, BECAUSE EITHER A TRANSACTION IS VOLUNTARY OR IT IS FORCED.

SINCE WHAT GOES AROUND COMES AROUND, IN THE LONG RUN, FORCE ENDS UP IN LOSE-LOSE RELATIONSHIPS. THEREFORE, NON-AGGRESSION LEADS TO WIN-WIN RELATIONSHIPS.

LIVE BY THE SWORD, DIE BY THE SWORD

AGGRESSION IN ITS EXTREME IS DEATH. AND THE REALITY IS THAT WE ALL DIE DESPITE HOW PEACEFULLY WE TRY TO LIVE OUR LIVES. IN OTHER WORDS, THE UNIVERSE AGGRESSES. AND SINCE THE UNIVERSE AGGRESSES, THE UNIVERSE AS A WHOLE IS A BIG LOSE-LOSE RELATIONSHIP.

WE ARE SLAVES TO THE LAWS OF PHYSICS AND MUST TOIL AWAY TO KEEP ENTROPY FROM TAKING OVER OUR PHYSICAL BODIES. NOTHING LASTS; THE UNIVERSE IS PROGRESSIVELY CONSUMING ITSELF INTO A HYPOTHETICAL DEATH. THE SURVIVAL OF THE FITTEST IS REALLY JUST A RACE TO THE BOTTOM.

CONSEQUENTLY, NON-AGGRESSION CAN BE REGARDED AS AN APPEAL TO A HIGHER ETHOS THAN THAT OF NATURE. NON-AGGRESSION IS AN APPEAL TO WHAT COULD BE REFERRED TO AS THE DIVINE IN US.

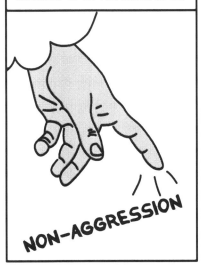

NON-AGGRESSION

PSYCHOLOGICALLY, THE RULES ARE DIFFERENT THAN PHYSICALLY. WE CAN THUS MAKE RELATIONSHIPS PSYCHOLOGICALLY WIN-WIN REGARDLESS OF WORLDLY ENTROPIC LOSE-LOSE LIMITATIONS.

EVEN THOUGH HUMANS NEED TO EAT, WHICH INEVITABLY ENTAILS AGGRESSION, WE'VE LEARNED TO AT LEAST GROW AND RAISE FOOD IN WAYS THAT CREATE SOMEWHAT WIN-WIN RELATIONSHIPS.

AS OPPOSED TO LOSE-LOSE LIKE EARLY AMERICANS ALMOST DRIVING THE BUFFALO INTO EXTINCTION.

MANY CROPS AND CERTAIN BREEDS OF ANIMALS DEPEND ON HUMANS TO STAY ALIVE AND THRIVE AFTER ALL. AND SINCE ALL THINGS DIE ANYWAY, AS PAYMENT, WE MAKE A MEAL OUT OF OUR EFFORTS OF GROWING CROPS AND RAISING ANIMALS.

SINCE PLANTS AND ANIMALS DON'T TALK, WE CAN'T REALLY DECIPHER WHETHER OR NOT THEY CONSENT TO OUR RELATIONSHIP WITH THEM. BUT UNTIL THEY RISE UP AND RESIST, IT IS NOT UNREASONABLE TO BELIEVE THAT THEY ACCEPT OUR RELATIONSHIP.

I'M ON A HUNGER STRIKE. I'M ONLY EATING ENOUGH TO STAY ALIVE.

THE SAME COULD BE SAID OF THE RELATIONSHIP BETWEEN HUMANS AND GOVERNMENT. IF ALL THAT HUMANS CAN DO IS FIGHT OVER WHAT KIND OF GOVERNMENT THERE SHOULD BE, THEN THEY OBVIOUSLY ACCEPT THAT THERE SHOULD BE GOVERNMENT--AND ALL THE SELF-CONTRADICTING FORCE THAT COMES ALONG WITH IT.

TEAR GAS

THEIR SLAVERY DOESN'T HAVE TO BE YOUR SLAVERY THOUGH. YOU DON'T HAVE TO GO THROUGH OTHERS TO GET FREEDOM. SO, DON'T DESPAIR AND ACCEPT IT AS TRUE THAT OTHERS CAN CONTROL YOUR FREEDOM.

NOT EVEN THE LAWS OF PHYSICS CAN STOP YOU FROM BEING FREE. FREEDOM IS A STATE OF MIND. AND WHEN YOU CAN LEARN TO ACCEPT NON-AGGRESSION IN YOUR MIND, YOU WILL AUTOMATICALLY ACCEPT IT IN THE WAY YOU LIVE.

GENERALLY, PEOPLE ARE PRIMARILY ENSLAVED BY THEIR OWN AGGRESSION AGAINST WHAT IS BEYOND THEIR DIRECT CONTROL.

IS THIS FREAKING LIGHT EVER GREEN?

FOR EXAMPLE, I CAN CONTROL EATING AN APPLE BECAUSE APPLES ARE AVAILABLE TO ME. BUT I CAN'T QUITE CONTROL THE QUALITY OF AN APPLE I EAT. NOT ALL APPLES TASTE VERY GOOD.

SO, IF I AGGRESSED AGAINST THE REALITY THAT ALL THE APPLES I HAVE AVAILABLE TO ME ARE MEDIOCRE, I'D JUST BE ENSLAVING MYSELF TO AN IDEAL BEYOND MY DIRECT CONTROL. EVEN IF I STARTED MY OWN APPLE ORCHARD, I'D STILL BE SUBJECT TO THINGS BEYOND MY CONTROL LIKE THE WEATHER.

SIMILARLY, I CAN CONTROL BUYING SOME SHARES OF A CERTAIN STOCK AT A SET PRICE. HOWEVER, WITHOUT THE ABILITY TO MANIPULATE THE STOCK PRICE, I CAN'T CONTROL WHERE THE PRICE OF THE STOCK GOES. IF I AGGRESSED AGAINST THE REALITY THAT THE STOCK I BOUGHT IS GOING DOWN IN PRICE, I'D JUST BE ENSLAVING MYSELF TO AN IDEAL BEYOND MY CONTROL.

THOSE DAMN WALL STREET CROOKS ALWAYS KNOW HOW TO SUCKER A GUY IN RIGHT AT THE TOP!

IT IS PSYCHOLOGICAL AGGRESSION TO DEMAND THAT THINGS BEYOND YOUR DIRECT CONTROL BE A CERTAIN WAY.

IF YOU CANNOT ENJOY THE PURSUIT OF SOMETHING BEYOND YOUR DIRECT CONTROL, EVEN IF IT IS ULTIMATELY FRUITLESS, THEN YOU ARE ENSLAVING YOURSELF.

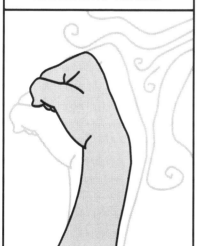

YOU HAVE TO TAKE THE BASIC ATTITUDE OF: I MAY HAVE A PREFERENCE, BUT I ULTIMATELY DON'T GIVE A DAMN BECAUSE IT IS BEYOND MY DIRECT CONTROL. I'M NOT GOING TO SHAKE MY FISTS OF AGGRESSION AT THE WIND.

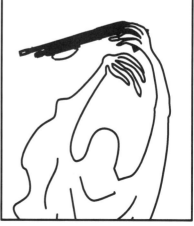

THAT APPLIES TO GOVERNMENT JUST AS MUCH AS IT DOES TO ANYTHING ELSE. IF YOU AGGRESS AGAINST THE GOVERNMENT, YOU ARE JUST MAKING IT REAL AND ENSLAVING YOURSELF TO A GHOST THAT WILL PROBABLY AGGRESS RIGHT BACK.

AGAIN, FREEDOM IS A STATE OF MIND. AND WHEN YOU CAN LEARN TO ACCEPT NON-AGGRESSION IN YOUR MIND, YOU WILL AUTOMATICALLY ACCEPT IT IN THE WAY YOU LIVE.

AGGRESSION, WHETHER IT IS PHYSICAL OR MENTAL, IS LIKE TAKING POISON HOPING SOMEONE ELSE WILL DIE.

INITIATION OF FORCE IN A BOTTLE

WARNING: POISON

SO, KEEP IN MIND THAT TO CONDEMN FOOLS IS TO CONDEMN YOURSELF TO THE SAME FOOLISHNESS OF THOSE YOU CONDEMNED AS FOOLS.

IT ALL LOOPS AROUND, AND NON-AGGRESSION IS THE TICKET OUT OF THAT LOOP.

PEACE

NON-AGGRESSION

111111

AGGRESSION IS ULTIMATELY THE SLAVE AND MASTER GAME. THE MASTER IS A SLAVE TO HIS SLAVES. HAVE NO SLAVES AND YOU WILL BE FREE. THAT IS THE LITERAL MORAL OF THIS STORY.

SO ANYWAY, I HOPE YOU ENJOYED THIS BOOK.

LOOK INSIDE

BEYOND THE GOVERNMENT-HUANTED WORLD (PAPERBACK)

ZANDER MARZ (AUTHOR)

★★★★★

PRICE: TOO EXPENSIVE TO SHOW

IN STOCK

- -

CUSTOMER REVIEWS

IF YOU DIDN'T LIKE THIS BOOK, THEN THE REALITY IS THAT YOU'D RATHER SET UP THE CONDITIONS FOR YOUR OWN DESTRUCTION UNDER THE GUISE OF SOME GILDED DELUSION OF ORDER BY FORCE.

YOU DON'T NEED TO BELIEVE ME, JUST SET DOWN THE GUNS, SET DOWN THE FORCE, AND WE'LL SEE WHO'S RIGHT.

REALISTICALLY, IF YOU DON'T BELIEVE ME, I'D VENTURE TO SAY THAT THE ONLY THING GOING FOR WHAT YOU MAY BELIEVE OTHERWISE IS THAT IT IS BACKED UP BY FORCE.

AND IF THAT IS YOUR STANCE, YOU ARE BASICALLY GIVING ME AND EVERYONE ELSE A GREEN FLAG TO INITIATE FORCE ON YOU.

INITIATE FORCE

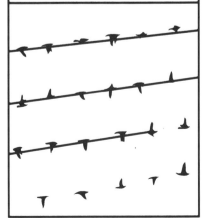

SO, BEFORE YOU GO MAKING A FOOL OF YOURSELF TRYING TO DISMISS THESE IDEAS, TAKE A HARD LOOK AT THE UTTER INSANITY YOU ARE DEFENDING. DO YOU REALLY WANT TO GO DOWN IN HISTORY AS SOMEONE WHO BELIEVED IN BARBAROUS GHOSTS AND SUPPORTED FREE-RANGE SLAVERY?

PEACE.

BEYOND THE GOVERNMENT-HAUNTED WORLD

INDEX OF REFERENCES

THIS IS A LIST OF PEOPLE WHOSE SPECIFIC IDEAS, SPOKEN WORDS, OR WRITINGS WERE DIRECTLY CITED AND USED IN THIS BOOK.

1 STEFAN MOLYNEUX: VARIOUS IDEAS PULLED FROM THE FREE DOMAIN RADIO, AKA STEFBOT, YOUTUBE CHANNEL. STEFAN WAS PROBABLY THE BIGGEST INFLUENCE IN MAKING ME WANT TO MAKE THIS BOOK. THE INSIGHTS STEFAN PROVIDED PROVED TO ME TO BE THE MISSING LINK I NEEDED TO PUT TOGETHER A BOOK LIKE THIS. AND I SHOULD ALSO MENTION THAT IT IS THANKS TO JEFF BERWICK THAT I EVER STARTED PAYING ATTENTION TO STEFAN IN THE FIRST PLACE.

2 ROBERT ANTON WILSON: ZEN STORY FROM THE BOOK *PROMETHEUS RISING*.

3 DAMON VRABEL: RENAISSANCE 2.0 VIDEO.

4 MURRAY ROTHBARD: USED THE WORDING OF HIS DEFINITIONS TO DERIVE DEFINITIONS FOR CONCEPTS LIKE CUSTOMERISM.

5 JEFFREY TUCKER: REFERENCED SOME OF HIS RECORDED DISCUSSIONS ABOUT INTELLECTUAL PROPERTY.

6 YOUTUBE CHANNEL LORAX2013 VIDEO "WHY YOU ARE A SLAVE & HOW TO BECOME FREE."

7 STEPHEN HAWKING: LECTURE GÖDEL AND THE END OF PHYSICS.

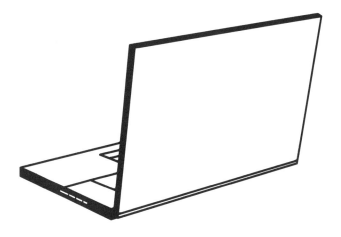

VISIT ONLINE
WWW.INSPIREDARTSPRESS.COM/ZANDERMARZ

FOLLOW AND LIKE
BEYOND THE GOVERNMENT-HAUNTED WORLD
ON FACEBOOK

22442794R00103

Made in the USA
Lexington, KY
28 April 2013